The Good Religion:
The Occidental Temple of the Wise Lord

Darban-i-Den

Published by
LODESTAR
P.O. Box 16
Bastrop, Texas 78602

www.seekthemystery.com

Contents

Abbreviations

CE	Common Era (= A.D.)
BCE	Before the Common Era (= B.C.)
Av.	Avestan
Phl.	Pahlavi (= Middle Persian)
MP	Modern Persian
Y.	Yasht
Ys.	Yasna

Note on Technical Terminology

Technical Mazdan religious terminology is drawn from many different languages— Avestan, Pahlavi, New Persian and Gujurati, all of which reflect the long and varied history of the religion over time and space. Occasionally the forms of the technical terms have been selected for their ease for the modern English speaker to pronounce and remember them. It seems that modern Zoroastrians have become comfortable with a kaleidoscope of languages for the technical terms in their religion. Although English equivalents or translations could be used, certain technical terms are necessary for precise communication and thought.

Acknowledgments

Thanks go to Michael Moynihan for his reading and correcting of the manuscript and to Don Webb for his reading and insightful questions.

A Personal Journey

In May of 2013 I announced to a small gathering my intention to form a "church" dedicated to the Wise Lord. This came as a shock to some. Others were puzzled. A few understood my meaning. What even fewer knew was that this announcement was the result of a long process of development and the inspired application of certain logical and philosophical principles. This institution is dedicated to the Wise Lord, known in Avestan as Ahura Mazda. Philosophically this is the principle of pure, focused consciousness. This idea is basically the standard understanding of who and what Ahura Mazda is, as established by Zarathustra.

Over the years several individuals had led me to greater inner knowledge of the teachings of the ancient Iranian prophet Zarathustra. These were sometimes directly intentional communications and at other times they were indirect and unintentional. These experiences are more marked by the effect they had on me rather than the outward drama of the encounter.

The first of these occurred in 1971 when I was an eighteen-year-old student at a language school in Germany. One of my fellow students was a certain "Herr Ahmadi" who worked as an information officer in the government of the then-reigning *Shahanshah* (emperor or more literally "king of kings") of Iran. He was very enthusiastic about both the past and future of Iran. I was young and knew very little about most things at the time. But it was his clear intimation in all that he said that the Shah was to return his country to its former position as a world leader and that this would be done by returning her to her past glories.

Just a few years later, after I had learned more of Zoroastrianism, I had a vivid dream of being in the presence of the Shah and I exhorted him to return to the faith of his ancestors. Did he continue to move in that direction to the end?

Four years after this dream the Shah was deposed by a peanut farmer who allowed the Ayatollah to reverse the gains made in Iran and return her not to the glories of her distant past, but to the squalor of her more recent past imposed by a foreign conqueror: Arabic Islam.

Exactly ten years after my encounter with "Herr Ahmadi" I again found myself in Germany. This time I was doing doctoral research in ancient Germanic culture. A neighbor of mine turned out to be Shapur Shahbazi, a renowned historian and archeologist from Iran. He had most recently been the chief archeologist on the Persepolis project. With the Islamic Revolution of 1979 he found himself in trouble as a loyalist to the Shah. He was charged with various crimes, including "allowing cats to sleep in his bed." Luckily Dr. Shahbazi was exiled rather than imprisoned. In several meetings with Dr. Shahbazi he communicated to me the essence of Zoroastrian ideas. He was a great man, whose accomplishments were so significant for his country that after his untimely death in 2006, the government of the Islamic Republic of Iran allowed his body to be interred in the Tomb of Hafez complex in his native Shiraz. This honor is bestowed only on the greatest cultural heroes.

One of the most important influences on my own development was my nine-year period of study under the great Indo-Europeanist, Edgar Polomé. This study clearly taught me that the best truth is to be sought where we come closest to the *source* of things. Each national or tribal tradition constitutes a door opening inward toward the source in the middle— the principles of Indo-European culture, religion and myth. Access to the center only becomes available after one passes though several of these doors. All doors are theoretically equal, but the center transcends them all. Once one has accessed the center, one can begin to teach from that perspective. The doors I entered, each more or less deeply, were those o the Germanic peoples, the Celts, the Romans, Greeks, Slavs, Vedic Indians and Iranians.

Over a period of thirty years I absorbed more and more of the Way of the Wise Lord. I studied some Persian language, both Tajiki and Farsi dialects and dabbled in Avestan and Pahlavi. I thought that one day I would write a basic book on the subject of Zoroastrian religion.

In recent years I was exposed to many negative and depressing experiences: death of loved ones, illness of my beloved, my own aging, imminent threat of the destruction of my home by wildfire, betrayal by trusted people and general collapse of my life's work that I had spent forty years building up. In the midst of this my understanding of the Wise Lord grew. I did not reject any of my past allegiances as they were discovered to be adjuncts to the philosophy originally espoused by Zarathustra. I did not learn I had been wrong about those loyalties, but rather I had been incomplete in myself. I had not suffered the frailty of existence and learned to empathize with the downtrodden. In my efforts to pull myself up, I became a Nurse Aide, as the certification for that job was about the only way an old and over-educated man can get a job nowadays. In that work I confronted the Gates of Hell— life in the midst of the decay of the human mind and body. Such places are indeed the Halls of Ahriman. Some of the denizens of that world even recognized the little bit of Light I brought to their world: their eyes would get wide and their heads would go back and they would exclaim: "You're shining!" Others would take my hand and kiss it fervently. Of course it was not me personally causing these reactions, but the manifestation of what I sought: the Truth of the Wise Lord.

Over the years as I experimented with the practical ideas of Zoroastrianism I conducted a few "tests." After all the very word "magic" comes from the title of certain Zoroastrian priests. These tests were undertaken with the greatest respect, and I am sure that the Wise

Lord was aware of what was in my heart as I undertook each of the experiments. The purpose of these was to "prove" to myself that the traditional construct of Ahura Mazda had some sort of special power.

My initial experiment, done several years ago, involved changing something in my own mind. I had seen a film when I was younger which contained some disturbing scenes of animal cruelty. For some reason, if I ever thought of these scenes, I would have a visceral reaction and be upset for an hour or so afterward, I could not explain my reaction, it was quite irrational, as I had seen worse before and had no trouble shaking it off. The "problem" was in my own mind. Anyone who has tried to change something within their own minds will empathize that it seems as if should be the easiest thing to do, but in fact it often proves quite difficult. It can sometimes be impossible. So, I thought, the god of pure mind, historically and traditionally conceived of as such for almost four millennia should be able to fix a part of that thing (mind) of which he is the absolute manifestation. With sincerity I made contact with the name (Ahura Mazda), and prayed that this feeling or reaction be removed from my mind. An hour or so later I tempted the system and thought of the scenes in question. They flowed across my mind, but my emotions did not react as they had before. To this day that change has been permanent.

Another time, more recently, after I had learned my first Avestan formula: *Jasa me avanghe Mazda!*, "Come to my aid, O Mazda!" I had a job in which I had to pass a certain test to retain the position. It was tough for me, so I asked for the aid of Mazda with this formula, which I recited from memory three times. Within a matter of seconds a coworker, with a blank stare on his face, handed me a piece of paper and said: "These are the answers to the test." Now this was cheating, and not an honest thing to do, I confess. But I see it as a direct manifestation of the power of these formulas and of Ahura Mazda. I have used that and other Avestan formulas to similar effect without fail. It should be remembered, however, that these formulas are not to be abused. I was receiving demonstrations of their raw power, but the underlying message of the whole system is that we should do Good for its *own sake* and not for direct practical result. The great secret is, however, that if one can truly, consciously and honestly do the Good for the Good's sake, untold bounty will come your way.

These experiences were just small "miracles" meant to teach me that I was on the path of Truth. This book may be your first step in making the same journey, along your own pathways of discovery.

Stephen E. Flowers
March 20, 2014

Introduction

This book is intended to introduce the basic beliefs and practices of the Way of the Wise Lord, a Western form of the Mazdan religion. It will allow the individual to engage in religious activity on his or her own, to affiliate with the Occidental Church of the Wise Lord, and open the way to deeper understanding and insight.

A book of this sort is necessary because no such approach has ever been taken before. The Eastern branch of the religion, commonly known as Zoroastrianism, is not generally open to conversion by outsiders. There may be no more than 250,000 Zoroastrians in the world today. These numbers are dropping. We do not seek to convert to this religion, as it has been developed and maintained by certain cultural groups who wish to remain separate from outside influences. This is something they should continue to maintain. We would support them, and do what we can to aid in their survival. Our way is our own way which has been inspired by the principles of the Good Religion, or the *Beh-Dîn*, as it is known in Persian. Our path is our own path, which takes into account our own Western history, culture and needs. Some of our beliefs and practices might be found to be heretical to orthodox Zoroastrians, but I am sure that most will realize that we are moved by the spirit of the Wise Lord and that the differences are born of varying cultural and spiritual needs.

The time has come for the Way of the Wise Lord to once more be promulgated to the world, as the prophet Zarathustra first intended. His original universal vision was intended to transform the whole world, but it was stolen and twisted by others over the millennia to suit their own ends— domination and manipulation. We will learn that the Good Religion can only spread from one heart to the next in all good conscience. Coercion, force or violence should play no part in the process. Most universal religions have propagated themselves using these negative techniques. This book seeks to reverse the trend. We want to open the hearts and minds of those who read it to the values of the Good Religion. Our work is to make this faith once more a growing and spreading one. Now more than ever the world needs the good thoughts, good words and good deeds promoted by this religion. We may well be in the final stages of the second of the three cosmic ages foretold by Zarathustra— a time of battle between the forces of good and evil. In this phase the best among us, stimulated by the prevalence of the effects of destructive influences in our world, must rise up first within themselves, and then in the world, to think, communicate and act on behalf of the Good Religion. In so doinig they will help those ensnared in the nets of decay to remember the Truth.

The first part of this book provides some basic historical context for the very idea of the Good Religion and shows that although this may have arisen in Central Asia, it is really so ancient that it shares values and structures with all other Indo-European cultures spanning from India to Ireland. The second part of the book provides the basic ideas and beliefs of the Good Religion. These can be adapted and adopted into anyone's current belief structure in order to transform and improve it. Even if the tenets presented here only influence the direction and content of your present faith, we will just be repeating what has been the age-old history of the message of Zarathustra. No one has heard it who has not been affected by it. The third part of the book actually provides ritual and ceremonial activities you can do to show to yourself the power of the faith of the Magians— what real magic is all about and what it has always been about. By enacting these spiritual exercises you will confront the Truth in your own heart and gain more Insight (Av. *Daena*). You will then be prepared to enter the Occidental Temple of the Wise Lord.

We are engaged in a great new adventure. This is a journey of world-transformation. It requires the cooperation of hundreds of talented people in leadership roles to make it work. We need artists, philosophers, ritualists, musicians, mystics, astrologers, culinary specialists, architects, linguists, media specialists, designers, fund-raisers, gardeners, pyrotechnicians, IT-specialists, craftsmen and craftswomen of all sorts. But most of all we need men and woman dedicated as warriors for the eternal cause of the Wise Lord.

As you can see our purpose is no small one. We aim to fulfill the ancient prophecies of a light flashing from the east to the West and to introduce a viable form of the Good Religion to Western culture for the first time. Why has it taken so long, in a Western world starved for "something new," for the Magian Way to enter our culture in a pure way? The answer can only be that the time was not right until now, and that the Wise Lord simply prevented it from happening until the right time. Now is the time. This book is a sign and your own mission will become clear as you immerse yourself in the history, ideas and practices of the Good Religion. This can be the instrument for the transformation of the world into its final victorious state. Your thoughts, words and deeds from this point forward can bring us all closer to the time of Making-Wonderful.

HISTORICAL

Chapter 1
Historical

It is not necessary to know a great deal of history in order to practice the Good Religion. Its teachings stand on their own and are valid in and of themselves. They do not need to be justified or defended by historical arguments. The teachings are practical and eternal in their values. History is merely a contextual exercise. We can learn more about how the ideas came to be, and learn something of the human beings who are at the roots of the faith. This provides texture and context. Some, however, will find the historical aspects of extreme importance, and so we place it here at the beginning.

The Indo-Europeans

The Indo-European world is the root of our own present-day culture. For many this is a strange concept. Some have never even heard of "Indo-Europeans" before. This is because the medieval Church in the West did all it could to eradicate all knowledge of our true heritage. We share our primeval culture of language and ideas with those living in India and Iran as well as the well-known nations of Europe, the Germanic peoples (including the English), the Celts (Irish, Scots and Welsh), Italians, Greeks and Slavs. It is important to understand that the roots of the Good Religion are ones that we all share. We are part of the same primeval culture to which Zarathustra belonged all those thousands of years ago. This is in contrast to the culture of the ancient Hebrews with which we share no common root. The idea of Mesopotamia as the "cradle of civilization" is one promoted by the medieval Church. Our culture's deepest roots, as we shall see, lie in the region north of the Caucasus Mountains, between the Black and Caspian Seas.

We cannot hope to treat this idea comprehensively in a book of this kind. I would refer the reader to the section "Indo-European and the Indo-Europeans" in any recent edition of the *American Heritage Dictionary*. Nevertheless, it is important to understand the most ancient cultural context which gave rise to the priest Zarathustra's prophetic insights.

The Indo-Europeans, more "romantically" referred to as "Aryans," probably had their origins around 5,500 BCE. At least the testimony of archeology would seem to suggest this. A culture existed at that time in the region north of the Caucasus in an area of steppe-lands bordered by deep forests to the north. Some say they originally migrated to this region from even father north... More importantly we can say that some fairly tight-knit group of these people spoke a language which linguists call Proto-Indo-European. This language coalesced around 4,500 BCE, and it was about this time also that they began their further migrations. These migrations would eventually take them all around the world. They entered what is present-day Turkey and became the Hittites, they entered Europe where they became the Celts, Germanics, Italics, Hellenics (Greeks), and Slavs. Another group, the Indo-Iranians, at first stayed close the original homeland and then moved southward and to the east around the time of 1,700 to 1,300 BCE.

While still in the homeland these people used a term related to the word "Aryan" to identify themselves. The word is the same root found in the term *Ir*-an and *Ire*-land, or the Germanic *Ir*-men. Technically "Aryan" refers only to the Indian branch, but it was adopted by the West as the best example of the self-identification of these people, our most distant cultural ancestors.

Through a combination of linguistics and archeology we know a good deal about the culture of these Aryans. If there is a word for something derived form a common root in Sanskrit, Greek and Gothic, for example, then it must mean that this word and the object or idea that it denotes were present before the languages went their separate ways over time and space. Using these methods we can know that the Indo-Europeans lived in an area where it snowed, were in lands which were part steppe and part forest. This forest included birch trees, which only grow north of a geographical line. They had domesticated the horse and used the wheel attached to wagons used for hauling goods as well as for war. They herded cattle and sheep. They transported themselves across and along waterways (rivers, lakes, seas). They smelted bronze and copper. The Hittites were among the first to smelt iron. They had patrilineial kinship patterns, that is, they identified themselves as the son or daughter of their father. Although they practiced agriculture, grew grains and used the plow, they could also have a nomadic or semi-nomadic existence riding horses, herding cattle and raiding the cattle of their neighbors. Some of them were rather like the cowboys of Central Asia.

These people were ideologically quite sophisticated and possessed a complex mythic and social structure. They had a system of sacrifice and poetic compositions to be sung to empower their sometimes rather elaborate rituals. The world of the gods was reflected in that of humanity and our temporal existence. Theirs was a tripartite, or three-fold, system. In this system there existed certain *functions*. The names of the gods and goddesses was less important than the system of functions which they fulfilled.

6

I. Judge-King : Poet-Magician	Sovereign Power
(cognitive) (intuitive)	
II. Warrior	Physical Power
III. Farmer/Craftsman	Re/productive Power

Society was arranged in this structure because the heavenly world of the gods was so arranged. This world is seen as a reflection of that one. The gods and goddesses were distributed in this structural model. Here we see a comparative model showing the Vedic Indian, Iranian, Germanic, and Roman systems.

Functions	I	II	III
Vedic	Mitra : Varuna	Indra	Aśvinau
Iranian (Zoroastrian)	Asha : Vohu Manah (order) : (good mind)	Khshathra (physical force)	Haurvatat : Ameretat (health) : (immortality)
Germanic	Týr : Óðinn	Thorr	Freyr : Njördr Freyr : Freyja
Roman	Dius Fidius : Iupiter	Mars	Quirinus : Ops

Many of the Indo-European groups had professional priests responsible for the performance of sacrifices. This was true of the ancient Celts and Italics as well as the Indo-Iranians.

Map I: The Original Homeland of the Indo-Europeans

● Area of the original homeland of the Indo-Europeans
➡ Major routes of Indo-European migrations

Map II: The Extent of Indo-European Expansion

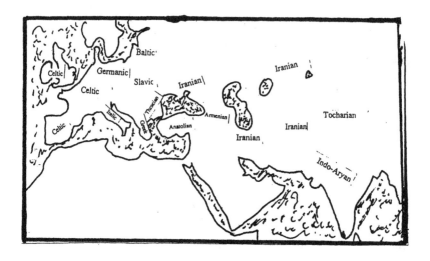

To summarize, the Indo-European world was once a closely knit group of tribes which lived in the Central Asian region. The first great division between them was that the Hittites split off and that a number of them moved westward into what is today Europe. Others went eastward to Iran and India. But they all remain brothers, even today, and even if they have long since forgotten who their bothers are. Part of our work is to find a way in which we can rediscover our long lost brothers.

The Indo-Iranians

In the eastern part of the Aryan world dwelled the Indo-Iranians. At first these people were very closely related, but they began to drift apart around 1,700 BCE. For our purposes it is only important to realize that these groups were exemplary models of the Indo-European tradition shared by the European West— really part of one whole. Also, it is crucial to know that these two groups were ideologically very similar at the time of their split. Some of the Iranians took a more westerly path south of the Caspian Sea, once they left central Asia, others remained in their eastern homeland, east of the Oxus River, while others headed in a northwesterly direction north of the Black Sea. The Indo-Aryans went in a southeastern direction and entered what is today Pakistan and northern India.

The original similarity of these two groups is exemplified in the liturgical languages of the two groups. In eastern Iran the ritual language is known as Avestan (from the word *Avesta*, the holy books of the Zoroastrians, preserved in that language) while in India we have Vedic Sanskrit, in which the *Rig Veda* is recorded. The close relationship between these two languages can be seen by comparing the Sanskrit translation of an early Iranian hymn to the god Mithra/Mitra:

Avestan	Sanskrit
tam amavantem yazatem	*tam amavantam yajatam*
surem damohu sevistem	*suram dhamasu savistham*
mithrem yazai zaothrabyo	*mitram yajai hotrabhyah*

This powerful strong god Mithra
strongest in the world of creatures
I will worship with libations.

One does not have to be a scholar of these two languages to see the close similarity between the two texts.

The cultic practices of the Iranians at this time were also probably virtually identical to those of the Vedic Aryans. They were entirely polytheistic with many gods and goddesses vying for the attentions of the priests and people. It was within this religious milieu that Zarathustra was born. Plurality remained the hallmark of "pagan" Aryan belief and practice. These continued to develop in a straight line of descent and today are manifest in the Hindu religion of India.

The Iranians

Now we want to turn our attention to the specific branch of the Aryans which gave rise to the Prophet Zarathustra and which provided the cultural matrix for the development of the religion which is his legacy. This is only intended as a brief survey of Iranian cultural history up to the time of Firdowsi.

The ancient Iranian world is divided into three major cultural spheres. These are commonly called the eastern, northern and western realms. It is the eastern area that Zarathustra was born, lived and died. The eastern sphere, with its unique dialect of language, called Avestan, disappeared from history as it was subsumed by the western Iranian Empire. The northern branch continued its archaic Indo-European horse-based lifestyle and gave rise to tribes such as the Scythians, Sarmatians and Alans. All of these played roles in the history of Europe. The western Iranians entered the area now occupied by the modern nation of Iran or the Iranian Plateau around 2,000 BCE.

9

The Iranian Plateau has had a history of continuous civilization from about 4,000 BCE. The Iranian Peoples entered the region of present-day Iran beginning in dawn of the second millennium and 1,500 years later they had established three kingdoms in the region: the Medes in the northwest, the Persians in the southwest and the Parthians in the north. The region was at first politically dominated by the Assyrians (Mesopotamians) until the Medes unified with the Persians formed the first empire and won their independence. In alliance with the Babylonians they conquered the Assyrian Empire in 612 BCE. In 550 Cyrus the Great established the Achaemenid Empire and through military genius and skill in governance expanded the empire from Egypt to India. Cyrus is credited with being an ideal leader and one of the world's first champions of human rights. He was more loved than feared, and his vast and well-organized empire would last for almost two-hundred years. His capital city was at Pasargad, an engineered city designed to withstand major earthquakes. Other notable Persian emperors of the Achaemenid dynasty were Darius I, who built the city of Persepolis, and Xerxes I.

Map III: The Empire of Cyrus

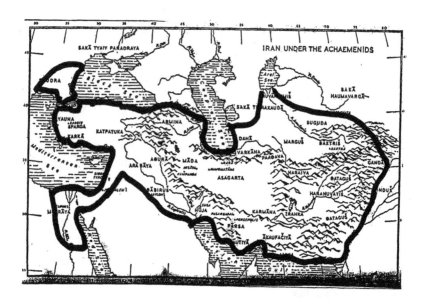

Persian conquests went all the way into the Balkans and the Greek islands in Europe. This led to conflict with the Greek city states which resulted in the Greco-Persian Wars (499-449 BCE). Conflict with the

10

Persians became a theme of Western politics from this time on. In 331 the Macedonian king, known to history as Alexander the Great, but among the Persians as "the Accursed Alexander," conquered the Persian Empire. In the process he destroyed much of the elaborate infrastructure that had been built up over the centuries and tried to kill off the Zoroastrian priesthood, thus mangling the record of religious oral literature. Shortly after his conquest, Alexander died and left chaos in his wake. The new empire was called the Seleucid, which was to last to 63 BCE. This empire was characterized by forceful and coercive attempts to Hellenize the Persians. Zoroastrianism was disestablished and had to survive underground.

A northwestern Iranian people, the Parthians, began mounting resistance to the Seleucids and eventually ousted them to renew an Iranian-based culture in the region of old Persia. Zoroastrianism was restored as a major religion of the new empire, although many other cults were also practiced.

In 224 CE the Prince of Persia, Ardashir, defeated the Parthians and became the new "King of Kings." This was the beginning of the Sasanian Empire. This empire was in every way comparable to the power and influence of the Achaemenid Empire. Zoroastrianism became its official religion and its cultural influence would be felt throughout the known world. This empire would last until the Arab/Muslim conquests of 642-664.

The Arab/Muslim conquest was a tremendous shock to Iranian culture. The Arabs had been minor players in the world until the rise of the religious zealotry and organized violence expressed by Mohammed and his followers. Persians had dominated all aspects of life between the Indus in the east and Mesopotamia in the west for six centuries. Persian was the language of commerce and Zoroastrianism was the gold standard of all religions. Soon after the Arabic conquest the Persians reasserted themselves from within Islam, providing the new faith with a philosophical depth and learning it had lacked before the Persians had been forced to accept it. The Persian language survived and thrived in the time to follow and was used for epic poetry, such as the *Shahname* of Firdowsi and the sufi poetry and philosophies of Hafez, Rumi and Omar Khayyam. Iran was Islamicized, but it was not Arabicized. Islam itself was transformed in Persian hands, it became what is called *Islam-e Ajam* (Islam of the [Non-Arab] Nations). It was the universalistic and philosophical nature of Iranian ideas that spread the new religion to the Turkic peoples to the north of Persia.

For most of the early history of the Iranian peoples there was a north/south divide. To the south were the civilized peoples and to the north were the barbaric horsemen. Those to the north are most often referred to with the umbrella term "Scythian." These northern Iranian tribes — really Scythians, Sarmatians and Alans — led nomadic lives.

11

They rode horses and drove chariots as did their most distant Indo-European ancestors. They lived on the wide-open steppe which stretched from present-day southern Russia into the heart of Central Asia. In many ways these were "barbaric" tribes. Little is known of their mythology or religion, although clear Iranian-Germanic mythic and symbolic correspondences seem to show something of the elements of their cosmology. Although the continued to worship the old Indo-European gods, they were probably also informed through the ideas of Zarathustra. As a distinct ethnic group these tribes almost completely disappeared from history by around 700 CE. But descendants of the Alans survive today in the Caucasus region as the Ossets, who still speak an Eastern Iranian dialect.

Iran and the World

Over the millennia Iranian culture interacted with a wide variety of other cultures and Persian tastes and ideas became widespread due to their quality and usefulness. Perhaps the root of this cultural outreach to the rest of the world lies in the concept that Zarathustra had an ideology made to be projected to each and every human being, regardless of their national or tribal affiliation. This universalism became a part of the Iranian national character.

The Northern World

Throughout European history the Northern Iranian tribes (the Scythians, Sarmatians and Alans) interacted productively and most usually cooperatively with the Celtic and Germanic peoples of northern and central Europe. They were adversaries to the Greeks, but for the most part maintained peaceful relations with them. The Greek historian Herodotus is our chief authoritative source for Scythian culture. There was a good deal of cultural exchange that went on among these various peoples. The Celts of central Europe had productive interactions with the Sarmatians, and since the Sarmatians entered central Europe about the time the Germanic peoples were forming their separate identity, it has been thought that the Sarmatian influence was a key to this process. Archaic Germanic ideas of aesthetics and many mythic elements certainly indicate some sort of close relationship between these peoples as early as 700 BCE. Some some of the Sarmatians and the Alans formed alliances with the Goths and Vandals that lasted for several centuries.

The Jews and Judaism

Cyrus the Great conquered Babylon and both absorbed many Babylonian features and greatly influenced the people there. Among the population in Babylon was practically the whole nation of Israel, which had been taken into the so-called Babylonian Captivity by the Babylonian king after he destroyed their temple in 686 BCE. Cyrus liberated the Jews and even repatriated them back to their homeland. He financed the rebuilding of their temple and had his scholars aid the Jews in reworking their religious documents. A number of Jews formed a pro-Persian faction. Some wanted to convert to the Good Religion, and no doubt some did. But this was not the purpose or intent of Cyrus, who followed the teachings of the Prophet regarding the non-use of coercion in matters of conscience.

From the time of Cyrus the Great, Jews began to immigrate to Persia itself. They could have returned to Israel, but they chose to follow Cyrus in Persia. Certain books of the Old Testament refer to the life of the Jews in Persia: Isaiah, Daniel, Ezra, Nehemiah, Chronicles and Esther. Judaism was greatly transformed by Persian influence. This was the origin of the split between the Saducees and Pharisees. Ideas of heaven and hell, angels, resurrection of the dead, the coming of a Savior, and most importantly the idea of the *universality* of God, all came into Judaism from the Zoroastrian philosophy. It must be said, however, that the synthesis of Judaic and Zoroastrian beliefs was not very thorough or in any way systematic one in Judaism. For example, although the *imagery* of the myth of the Garden of Eden in the Book of Genesis is taken from Zoroastrian lore (Paradise/Garden, Original Man and Woman, Serpent, etc.) the overall *meaning* of the story in Judaism and Zoroastrianism is different. The Good Religion does not have a doctrine of the Fall of Man from the Grace of God. Mazda wants mankind to become enlightened and to become "god-like" in nature. That is, he wants each individual to be united with all parts of his soul— to become whole and immortal. The Wise Lord is not jealous, fearful or wrathful, he is eternally loving, courageous and serene. He is the true God, not a demon.

The whole tradition of angels in Judaism is taken from Zoroastrian doctrine. The depth of this reality is brought home by the fact that the three archangels of Judaism: Michael, Gabriel and Rafael are actually arranged in the Indo-Iranian system of tripartition:

Michael = Like *God*
Gabriel = *Strong* as God
Rafael = *Healing* as God

Until the time of the Safavid dynasty, beginning in 1502, Iran and the Jews had a happy relationship. It was only in this early modern time that the Shi'ite hatred for the Jews became increasingly manifest. The government of the most recent Shah of Iran generally renewed the traditional friendship with Israel along with many other ancient ideas, all of which was fuel for the hatred of the mullahs toward him. There was a significant minority of Jews in Iran up to the events of 1979. Many Iranian Jews have since migrated to the United States.

Buddhism

Because Persian was the major language along the Silk Road, the caravan routes that transported goods from China and India to the Near East, this language and the ideas contained in it spread like wildfire. Persia and India were always in a close cultural exchange network. When the system of thought developed by the fifth-century Indian philosopher Gautama Siddhartha, known as the Enlightened One (Buddha), spread to China and eventually to Japan it was along a northern road which had its epicenter in what is today Afghanistan. It is widely thought that the basic idea of the Buddha, enlightenment through silent meditation, originated with insights gained by Zarathustra who says in the Gatha 43:15:

As divine and sacred have I recognized Thee, O Lord of Life and Wisdom, when Vohuman entered within me and light of Truth and knowledge brightened my heart. Then I *realized that silent and deep meditation is the best means of acquiring knowledge and spiritual insight,* and that it is not fit for any leader to make peace with the followers of untruth, because they regard righteous and truthful persons as their enemies.

Buddhism may have been sparked by the insights of Zarathustra. Siddhartha could have easily heard of the basic concept of a universal religious system based on simple principles and supported by a fundamental set of mental disciplines and ethics from any visiting Iranian. It is said that two traveling merchants from Iran named Tapassu and Bhallika heard the teachings of the Buddha directly and returned home to spread these teachings.

It was in the northern region where India and Iran came together in ancient times that a syncretism of Iranian and Buddhistic ideas gave rise to Mahayana Buddhism. Essential to this school is the idea of the Bodhisattva, one who is responsible for the salvation of others, a clear reflection of the Zoroastrian idea of the Saoshyant. One statue of Buddha has been found in this region inscribed as "Buddha-Mazda." The Buddhistic art of the area also shows clear Zoroastrian influence, with the Buddha being shown possessing the *khvarr*, as flames arising from his head and shoulders. One figure from Buddhist mythology of this region named Kshitigarbha conducts the souls of the dead across a "bridge of death," a clear reflection of the Chinvat Bridge, the mythic bridge in Iranian tradition over which the souls of the dead pass as they are judged by Daena according to the qualities of their deeds.

All vestiges of Buddhism were eradicated from the area by the conquering Muslims. The most recent act of their intolerance was carried out by the Afghani Taliban in 2001 when they destroyed two hundred-foot tall statues of the Buddha carved by their ancestors in the solid rock cliff-face in the Bamiyan Valley.

There are fundamental differences between the Good Religion and Buddhism. Chief among them is that the first of the Four Noble Truths of Buddhism is that "life is suffering," whereas the Good Religion sees this life as a joy, even if it is an often unrealized joy. Ignorance fostered by the Lie is the source of suffering.

The Greeks

Beginning around 600 BCE the Greeks began have direct and indirect contact with the Persians. Greeks traveled to Persia and the Persian Empire itself expanded to the very border of the Hellenic homeland. Although the Greeks and Persians were political and military rivals, the Greeks anxiously absorbed as much of Persian culture and learning as they could find. Pythagoras is said to have studied Zoroastrian teachings in Babylon, Other Greek philosophers credited Persia as the place where wisdom had its origins. Aristotle, tutor of Alexander the Great, stated that "the Magi are more ancient than the Egyptians," and "Zoroaster is the originator of wisdom." The Greeks were the Persians' greatest pupils. The Greeks more than any other people understood and absorbed the dramatic significance of Zarathustra's ideas. Greek philosophers and historians ascribed all sorts of ideas and practices to Persia. Some accurate some not. It is most likely the true philosophical impulse came to Greece from Persia. This came with the ideas that there is *one* source of divinity (the One, the Good, the Light), that all the gods are created by this Source, and that the other gods and goddesses are exponents of *abstract principles*. Once one realizes this fact, the human individual is transformed from a believer into a philosopher— a lover of wisdom.

After the conquest of Persia by Alexander there was a conscious policy of Hellenization, in which the Olympian gods and goddesses were officially worshipped. Over time these images were increasingly Iranianized, so that there existed for centuries a mixture of Greek and Iranian ideas and myths. It was only in the Parthian period that more purely Iranian ideas came to the forefront again. But it was from within this centuries-long Greco-Iranian synthesis that the Western cult of Mithras arose. This is a cult that would become a major force among the Romans. This same synthesis is the cauldron out of which Christianity and Manicheanism also emerged.

Christianity

The Occidental Temple of the Wise Lord teaches that Jesus was a Zoroastrian Saoshyant, or Savior. He taught the Magian principles as

15

best he could to the culture into which he was born. But his teachings were betrayed and corrupted by those who founded a religion in his name. Here we will see just a few of the ideas connected to this. A more extensive discussion of the Magian Jesus is found in our book *The Mazdan Way*.

The early organized Christian Church was founded by men who hated Jesus in life and who were never directly taught by him. These are James the brother of Jesus and Saul/Paul of Tarsus. The first would have nothing to do with Jesus and called him insane while he lived, the other one was a professional persecutor of Christians in the beginning. Any who followed the true teachings of Jesus were eventually relegated to an oblivion engineered by an organized system based on coercion and lies. Jesus had nothing to do with this coercion. It might be asked why no one seems to have followed the true teachings of the Master? Some tried, but they were wiped out over time by those using force and violence. The coercive system created by the early organized Church was so effective that its practitioners were seduced by the power they gained by using it and were quickly consumed by this addiction. This is to be contrasted with the history of Zoroastrianism, which had about two thousand years of history behind it before it ever even became an established state religion in Iran. At its best the Good Religion is a matter of conscience, not coercion.

Any objective observer can see that the religious systems of the so-called Old and New Testaments are very different from one another. Jesus seems to have taught an even more highly Persianized form of Judaism than the one represented by the Pharases, or "Persian faction" of the Judaism of his day. Jesus taught about a Heavenly Father God, to the Jews God is not their father, but their chief and master. The relationship to him is a contractual, not a familial one. The Jews are said to be "chosen" by God, but the Zoroastrians, like most Indo-Europeans, see the fatherhood of God. To the Indo-European God is family, not a contractual boss. Jesus' God is universal, the god of the Jews is tribal, a God that belongs to them, not to the world. Jesus taught love, the Jews followed the Law (*torah*). Jesus, like Zarathustra, taught about individual choice and individual salvation. The Jews saw the choice and salvation as a corporate thing. The people as a whole will be granted salvation, but not individuals before this final corporate event. Jesus taught the interiority of God, the "Kingdom of God is within you," while the Jewish conception was one of an exterior God. Christianity is not an extension of Judaism, it is an entirely different type of system.

There are many clues to the reality of this interpretation. One of the chief clues is to be found in the story of the so-called Three Wise Men. These were three Magian or Zoroastrian priests who, by astrological computations for which they were famous in the ancient world, had determined that a Saoshyant would be born in Israel at the time of the birth of Jesus. They came and visited him and acknowledged his role as a figure in their system. It is likely that he again made contact with them, and with the Magian Way, as a young man. Again this theory is borne out by the fact that so many of the sayings attributed directly to Jesus are paralleled in the Avestan texts of Zoroastrianism. Here are a few examples of many:

Jesus—	Zarathustra—
...for he makes his sun rise on the evil and on the good and sends rain on the righteous and on the unrighteous. (Matt. 5:45)	I realized you to be the seed of holiness, O Mazda, since yours are those arms with which you give protection and which you give blessings both to the good and to the bad. (Y. 43.4)
So I tell you whatever you ask for in prayer, believe that you have received it and it will be yours. (Mark 11:24)	And to those you know who on account of their righteousness and good mind are wise and upright, O Ahura Mazda, you will fulfill their desire by granting its attainment; for assuredly I know that devout prayers for righteous ends never remain unanswered by you. (Y. 28.10)
"Thy will be done..."	"Whatsoever He, in his wisdom thinks, ought to be..."
"The same from everlasting to everlasting"	"The same at every now."
"Do unto others as you would have them do unto you."	"That nature alone is good which shall not do unto another whatever is not good for its own self."

These could be multiplied many times over. The pre-existing influences of Zoroastrianism in Judaism makes the more fundamental and conscious mission of Jesus all the more understandable. Jesus in nothing less than a Saoshyant, and was recognized as such by the Three Magi. Saoshyants are supposed to appear approximately every thousand years. For these reasons the adherents of the Occidental Church of the Wise Lord study the words of Jesus.

The Arabs and Islam

Today Iran is known as one of the Islamic countries *par excellence*. It is perhaps second only to Saudi Arabia itself as a center of Islamic culture and politics. This has its roots at the beginning of Islam. Here we will see how Iran influenced Arabia before Islam existed, how it was instrumental in inspiring Mohammed, and how after the conquest all of Islam was to a certain extent recreated in the Persian image. Early Islam was as much Persian as it was Arabic. The underlying friction in national psyche of Iran — caused by the fact that Islam was introduced as a part of a conquest by a culturally inferior people — eventually bubbles up in the form of a separate sect of Islam, known as Shi'ism.

The land of the origin of Islam is roughly identical with the modern state of Saudi Arabia. The Arabs of Mohammed's time and region were largely polytheistic, semi-nomadic Bedouins. Literacy was known, but not widespread. Mohammed was himself a merchant involved in the caravan trade from the Indian Ocean to the Mediterranean. The trade routes, parts of which are known by the romantic name "the Silk Road," stretched from China and India in the East to the Mediterranean in the West. Almost all of this network of trade routes and periodic weigh stations were dominated by Persian culture and language. This is mainly because the old Persian Empire of Cyrus the Great covered this entire area. The interior of the Arabian Peninsula, the homeland of Mohammed was called *Arabia Deserta* by the Romans. No great power ever thought it worth conquering. The Arabic language was already heavily influenced by Persian and certainly Zoroastrian concepts and beliefs would have been known to the Arabs. There were known to be Zoroastrian fire-temples in the Mecca of Mohammed's time. Mohammed regarded Zoroastrians "people of the book." Persians were in the entourage of Mohammed from the beginning and some have said that he was taught by a Zoroastrian master, and it was he who was characterized as an angel who commanded the Prophet of Islam to "recite."

Regarding Iranian ideas in the foundation of Islam, one noted expert has summed up:

> Islamic beliefs in heaven and hell, a last judgment based on the weighing (*mizan*) of good and bad deeds, a bridge of death, and angels, as well as tendencies towards millenarianism, messianism, and apocalypticism, along with notions of ritual purity, have all been argued to have Iranian origins. ... The angels Harut and Marut (Qur'an 2:96) are reflections of the Zoroastrian Haurvatat and Ameretat.

(Foltz, 2004, p. 118)

After the initial shock of the conquest by the Arabs had been absorbed, the Persians set about reasserting their intellectual and spiritual dominance, but from *within* the system provided by Islam. The degree and level of Persian influence on subsequent Islamic culture can be seen in the words of Ibn Khaldun, himself a famous Arabic philosopher of the fourteenth century:

> It is a remarkable fact that, with few exceptions, most Muslim scholars both in the religious and intellectual sciences have been non-Arabs... The founders of grammar ... were of Persian descent. Most of the *hadith* scholars who preserved the traditions of the Prophet for the Muslims were Persians, or Persian in language and breeding because the discipline was cultivated in Iraq and regions beyond. Furthermore, all of the great jurists were Persians, as is well known. The same applies to speculative theologians and to most of the Qur'an commentators. Only Persians engaged in the task of preserving knowledge and writing systematic scholarly works. Thus the truth of the statement of [Mohammed] becomes apparent, "If learning were suspended at the highest parts of heaven the Persians would attain it." ... The intellectual sciences were also the preserve of the Persians, left alone by the Arabs, who did not cultivate them.
>
> (Quoted by Frye, 1975, p. 150)

The Persians did not have to form a separate type of Islam to assert themselves, they actually reformed the orthodox system itself to suit their culture. It is this fact that leads some in Iran today to believe the apparent absurd idea that they were not really conquered by the Arabs, but rather that the Persians absorbed and reshaped Islam in their image. Shi'ism, the sect that dominates Iran today, was not an Iranian invention, and it only became the dominant sect in the country much later in the seventeenth century.

The Muslims accepted all of the Persian apparatus of governance that the Sasanian Empire had possessed. The Arabs had conquered an empire, but had no experience in running one. So the Persians had to be used for the job. Islam, which means literally "submission," spread in an entirely military/political way. Muslim conquerors did not forcibly convert the conquered peoples to Islam, they first and only demanded the *submission* of the people and their leaders militarily, and only after then was the religion brought into the picture. The Muslims would just tax the non-Muslims at a higher rate, so that eventually, over time, people would gravitate toward being convinced of the "good sense" it made to convert to Islam.

19

The Persians were instrumental in spreading Islam to the Turkic peoples to their north. They adopted the "star and crescent moon" symbol which was an Iranian/Zoroastrian symbol seen on many coins of the Sasanian Empire.

Islam destroyed the home-base of eastern Zoroastrianism. Zoroastrians survive in Iran, but just barely. This is a far cry from the Zoroastrian-based culture of Iran which made it the hub of culture and intellectual achievement in the ancient world.

Chapter 2
Zarathustra and his Mission

Life of Zarathustra

One might say we know very little about the facts surrounding the life of the Prophet Zarathustra. However, if we stop and realize the man lived as many as four thousand years ago we know very much indeed. We have words that he himself composed, we know of his family and some of his activities. This knowledge was all handed down orally for many centuries before it was written down. The linguistic fact that the nature of the language used by Zarathustra comes from the time around the early part or the middle of the second millennium BCE shows better than anything else that he lived at this time.

The fact that we know he was a real living man, that we have his own words, and that the essence of his message has come down to us in a pure form is a testimony to his extraordinary power. No man who lived so long ago has had the ability to speak to us in the here and now so clearly and forcefully. What is the explanation for this extraordinary personal ability?

Tradition holds that Ahura Mazda consciously sent the *khwarr* (glory) of the prophet-to-be into the hearth-fire of his maternal grandfather, from there it entered his grandmother's body, and from her it entered his mother's body, where it dwelled. Her name was Dughdova. Demons attempted to kill her because they recognized the Wise Lord's plan to cause a prophet of the Good Religion to be engendered in the world. Dughdova's father sent her away for her protection to the house of the chief of the Spitaman family. There she met the son of the chief, Pourushaspa, and eventually married him. At that time the *khwarr* entered Pourushaspa as well. In a sacred ritual, Pourushaspa and Dughdova drank the juice of the *haoma*-plant mixed with milk. At that point the *khwarr* came together with the *fravashi* (guardian spirit) and *tanu* (physical form) of the prophet-to-be in his mother's womb. Again the demons tried to kill him and his mother. But they were warded off when Dughdova made offerings of wood, butter and meat to the hearth-fire. Henceforth she was surrounded by a radiance which protected her from all attacks.

When Zarathustra was born he laughed out loud. Most babies cry because they are caused to see their own mortality — an illusion sent by the Lie — but Zarathustra saw the Truth and reacted with joy.

All indications are that the place of Zarathustra's birth was somewhere around the Aral Sea.

In ancient Indo-European society it was normal for families to foster their children out to be raised early on by others. Pourushaspa, temporarily afflicted by bad judgment, fostered Zarathustra out to a priest who repeatedly tried to kill the little fellow. But in every instance the boy was protected by divine power.

Throughout his boyhood Zarathustra spoke out against what he saw as bad practices. The fact that he later refers to himself as having been a priest (*zaotar*) and that he was in fact able to compose verse in the style and language of the ritual conventions of the Indo-Iranian cult show that he was actually trained as a priest in the tradition against which he would formally and consciously rebel. This training would have taken several years to complete.

When he was fifteen years old Zarathustra asked his for his share of his father's cord or girdle (*kushti*) symbolizing his inheritance from his father. This Zarathustra tied around his waist, as he was instructed by the Good Mind (Vohu Manah).

Tradition holds that when Zarathustra was twenty years old he left his parent's home to search for the Truth. He wandered throughout the countryside for years.

It is said that Zarathustra married and had children.

During the spring-festival in his thirtieth year, Zarathustra went to the river Daitya to draw water for the strength-giving *haoma*-ritual. On the banks of the river there appeared to Zarathustra the shining form of the Good Mind (Vohu Manah). He was transported to the court of the Wise Lord and the Holy Immortals. It is said that when he came to twenty-four feet of these the light was so intense that his body cast no shadow. In this state Zarathustra began to ask questions, to seek the Truth. His questions were answered. He returned to this world transformed into the Prophet of the Good Religion. He preached his new teachings to all and everyone. But for ten years no one understood him. Finally a cousin heard and understood the meaning of the Prophet's words. After ten years the gate was opened to the world.

Zarathustra entered the court of King Vishtaspa where he gained the confidence of Queen Hutaosa. She and her husband ruled a small realm around the Oxus River. They listened to the teachings of the Prophet with increasing interest.

A story is told, known as the Legend of the Grain, about Zarathustra and King Vishtaspa and how the Prophet taught him.

One day the king was traveling through his country and he came upon a beautiful garden. He inquired of his minister what this place was. The minister replied it was the garden of the wise man known as Zarathustra. The king entered and saw groups of people discussing wondrous things freely. The king had Zarathustra brought before him, as he wanted to ask him for the answers to questions none of his priests could give him.

Zarathustra came before the king, but immediately asked to be excused to engage in his work in the garden, which could not be neglected. The king was very annoyed with this and demanded some sort of instruction from the wise man. Zarathustra reached into his satchel and presented the king with an ear of grain. He told the king that the grain had been his teacher, and that it could teach him many things.

The king departed and when he got back to his palace he put the grain in a golden box. Daily he would open the box and stare at the grain, hoping for it to speak to him or somehow magically teach him secrets. But no such events transpired.

Highly annoyed, the king returned to the sage some months later with the grain in the golden box and demanded to know what the grain was supposed to teach him. Zarathustra asked what would have happened if, instead of putting the grain in a golden box, he would have planted it so that it could receive food and water.

Together the king and sage reflected upon the possibilities. The grain had to be removed from the box and planted in the earth so that good things could flow toward it. The king realized that he had to change his environment and ground himself so that the good things of nature and the spiritual world could flow freely toward him so that he could grow in knowledge and understanding. The answers he sought were within him. He would listen, not just hear, he would observe, not just see. Instead of demanding answers from others he would develop his own mind and arrive at the answers through insight.

Of course, the king's old priests and advisors did not sit idly by. They plotted relentlessly against the Prophet and even tried to have him executed. At one point the king had Zarathustra imprisoned, but he was released and exonerated when the Prophet magically cured the king's favorite horse. Zarathustra cured each of the four limbs of the horse in exchange for four promises from the king. First, that the king should convert to the Good Religion; second, that the king's son should do the same; third, that the queen should also be converted; and finally, that the king should execute those who attempted to have him executed. These events are said to have occurred in the Prophet's forty-second year.

With royal patronage the teachings of Zarathustra and the Good Religion spread throughout the region. The practical results from following the teachings of the Prophet were manifested and planted a growing seed in the Iranian people and beyond. These teachings were not unopposed, however. Many among the Turanian people, a non-Iranian population, opposed the Prophet vigorously. In at the age of 77 years and forty days, the Prophet was murdered by such a Turanian on December 26 in Balkh, and it is said that he was entombed there.

Subsequent facts show that Zarathustra had established a strong school of thought and had many priests under his tutelage at the time of his death. Theirs was an entirely oral culture. Writing did not exist. They composed and taught their works to others who memorized them, and passed them on from generation to generation. This is exactly how the *Rig Veda* was passed on through the millennia in India as well.

Teachings of the Prophet

The ideas directly taught by Zoroaster can be partially recovered by reading the *Gathas*, certain verses in the *Avesta* which are in the most archaic language, and which are records of his own words composed around 1,700 BCE. These *Gathas* represent only a surviving fragment of what the Prophet actually composed and taught in his lifetime. Other teachings are reflected in later texts. Also as many other teachers grew in the spirit of his teachings throughout the centuries, they augmented his ideas from within the tradition of his revelation. We will look at the great body of Zoroastrian religious texts later.

The teachings of Zarathustra were much more radical than later came to be expressed in the religious system his teachings inspired. This is because his ideas were so revolutionary that many could not accept them in their purest form, so the older system gradually, but only in certain areas, reasserted itself. Zarathustra thought abstractly in such a way that the Wise Lord was seen as a pure construct of absolute focused consciousness and all the other gods and goddesses were seen as mere rays, or extensions (angels), of this Principle. Many of the old gods reasserted themselves through the popular will over the centuries, but only in ways that were generally in accord with the principles of the Good Religion. The Good Religion embodies the best of both the monotheistic and polytheistic systems. It recognizes the singular source of divinity in the form of the lord of focused consciousness, and also recognizes the necessity of a multiplicity of value centers which allows for creativity and diversity in the spiritual life of individuals.

Insight

One of the greatest messages of the Gathas is that an individual, through devotion and exercise of the virtues of Good Thoughts and Good Words can make contact with the Wise Lord and gain insight from him through the reception of the Good Mind (Vohu Manah). Zarathustra first had the idea of God's unity and character, then further sought out the revelation of the mystery of God's knowledge by the reception of the Good Mind.

Theology

In the Gathas Zarathustra himself provides a clear description of the Wise Lord. Ahura Mazda is wisdom (consciousness), he is the first principle, he is all-seeing (omniscient), eternal and the Creator of existence. Furthermore, he is good and powerful, but *temporarily* he is not *all*-powerful. God is growing in power all the time with the help of conscious inhabitants of his creations, who are seen as his friends. Zarathustra did not speak of the old gods in a positive way: He focused on the abstract Triad of Ahura Mazda–Asha–Vohu Manah: Wise Lord–Truth/Order–Good Mind.

Moral Dualism: The Choice

Duality in the relative cosmos of the present age is a manifest fact: there is good and evil, the constructive and destructive, the orderly and the chaotic, and, most fundamentally, the conscious (wise) and non-conscious (ignorant). Zarathustra teaches that each individual is constantly confronted with the choice between the good and the bad, between thought and ignorance. Zarathustra taught silent meditation (Y. 43.15) but his is not a pacifistic system, rather it is a virile and robust fight against what is wrong in the cosmos and on earth. This is done with the weapons of Good Thoughts, Good Words and Good Deeds, and the teaching of his ideas and methods to others. Final victory is guaranteed to the Good because it is consciousness and sees ahead, whereas the Lie is ignorance and doomed to failure.

Many today are put off by the idea that there are "forces of good" and "forces of evil" in the world. This is partially due to the relativistic age in which we live, but it is also in part due to the misunderstanding of what the Mazdan philosophy is actually saying. The angels and demons are not in actuality anthropomorphic entities going around looking to do good or evil acts. Rather they are both sets of abstract paradigms or patterns of thought, symbol and/or material existence which are either constructive with regard to human and animal happiness, or those which are destructive to these interests. To deny that such patterns exist, and that they affect our lives, is illogical.

Enlightenment

With himself as an example, man is taught that by consciously seeking reception of the Good Mind so that man will be enlightened and guided by it. Furthermore, the individual can have the Good Mind intervene on his behalf. Perseverance based on faith in these precepts will be rewarded. Chief among the rewards are Immortality and Integrity.

Ethics

Zarathustra speaks repeatedly of the centrality of the Seven Creations and most especially the "Soul of the Ox" (by which he means the whole of the beneficial animal creation and humanity. Those persons and things which benefit the Seven Creations are praised and those persons and things which harm them are condemned. Mankind is exhorted to seek the Good Mind and to be guided by it toward Good Thoughts, Good Words and Good Deeds. Those who have been enlightened are exhorted to teach the Good Religion to others (Y. 33.2).

Agency of Mankind

Humanity is a chief active agent in the "entire remaking of existence." (Y. 48, 30.9) The process of seeking enlightenment and receiving the material rewards of that enlightenment is not intended to serve the needs of the individual for his or her own sake alone, rather the strength and endurance are provided that the individual may become a better agent for the renewal of existence.

We can summarize the nature of Zarathustra's astounding accomplishments by stating that he was:

- The First Prophet of a Universal Monotheistic Religion
- The First Theologian
- The First Philosopher
- The Originator of the Ideas of Universal "Human Rights"
- The First Defender of the Oppressed
- The First Conscious Environmentalist
- The Originator of the Idea of Women's Rights
- The Originator of the Idea of Animal Rights
- The First to Discover the "Power of Positive Thought"
- The Originator of the Practice of Silent Meditation

26

Chapter 3
History of Zoroastrianism

As we have seen Zoroastrianism, or the Good Religion, sprang from the roots of the common Indo-European traditional cult, of which Zarathustra was a priest. The religion was born suddenly in the revelatory vision of one man. His systematic reformation of the old cult formed the new religion from that point forward.

The ancients called their faith *Mazda-yasna*, literally "wisdom-worship" or *Behdîn*, "the Good Religion," or more literally the "good *insight.*" Zarathustra called it *Daena Vanuhi*, "Good Conscience." The religion is only called "Zoroastrianism" by outsiders or when followers of the Good Religion want to make their identity clear to others. This religion has had a continuous and dramatic history since its founding. It became the single most influential religious philosophy known to man, and yet has in recent years slipped into virtual obscurity. This short history of the Good Religion should make the reasons for all of this clear. Clarity should also be gained as to why it is necessary for us to renew the strength of the Good Religion here in the West.

Zoroastrianism and its Literature

We know that Zarathustra was a priest of the Iranian cult. He was trained in the oral recital of verses to be performed during the sacrificial rituals. We know this because the verses he composed for his new vision were in the style of this kind of poetry. His own verses, called the Gathas, survive in only fragmentary form and they are imbedded in the larger body of work called the *Avesta*. The original vision of Zarathustra reflected in the Gathas (ca. 1700 BCE) shows that the Prophet wanted to eliminate the worship of other gods and goddesses and focus exclusively on Ahura Mazda. Other divinities were either relegated to a demonic status, or were seen as abstract extensions of Ahura Mazda. Zarathustra had some success in his lifetime converting kings and others to the faith, and in establishing a priesthood for his new religion to carry it forth into history.

Other material was composed at a later date. We know this because the language is of a later kind, although still basically the same as that used by Zarathustra. The language is called Avestan, after the text in which it is found. This later material was composed between 1000 and 500 BCE. In the later material old gods such as Mithra re-emerge as *yazatas*, "those worthy of worship." For a full thousand years Zoroastrianism developed in Iran and beyond its borders as a universal faith of conscience. It entered various royal courts and migrated to the western part of Iran among the Medes and Paris, but it was not the official or state religion. In the west a priest in this religion was known as a *magū*. From this title our words "magic" and "magus" are derived. Other cults based in the older tradition existed in Iran alongside of the new religion. In other words the old gods and goddesses of Iran continued to be worshipped in many places and there was continuous cross-fertilization between the old system and the new.

This situation went on for approximately a thousand years, during which time the canon of religious verbal records was established and continued to be passed on orally within the priesthood. From 614 to 334 BCE Iran was formed into the world's first great empire, first in the west under the Medes and then under Cyrus (Kuresh) the Great and his successors. That Zoroastrianism was the religion of the emperors is revealed in many Old Persian inscriptions. An example of which is:

𐎺𐏁𐎴𐎠 𐎠𐎢𐎼𐎷𐏀𐎭𐎠𐏃 𐎠𐎭𐎶 𐎧𐏁𐎠𐎹𐎰𐎡𐎹 𐎠𐎷𐎡𐎹

vašnā Auramazdāha adam xšāyaθiya amiy
by the greatness of Ahura Mazda, I am king

During the time of this empire-building, Zoroastrian texts continued to be orally composed, memorized and transmitted, fire-temples began to be built, and even some sub-sects of the religion began to form. But it cannot be said that Zoroastrianism was the official state religion in the sense that everyone had to convert to it in order to live in the empire: Far from it. The Achaemenian Empire was a wondrous patchwork of nationalities and religions all working in harmony, each maintaining their own individualities.

In 334 disaster stuck when the Macedonian Alexander the Great conquered the Achaemenian Empire and in a barbarous fashion laid waste to significant amounts of Iranian culture and its resources— secular and religious. Priests were killed and temples sacked. Alexander died shortly thereafter. The Greeks created a Hellenized system of religion which brought together Hellenic and Iranian elements. In 312 BCE the Seleucid Empire was established, which was Hellenistic in character. Under Greek influence the Zoroastrians began to develop a script with which to write down the remnants of the religious material. Zoroastrians had to retreat to the mountainous areas to survive the process of Hellenization. When the Seleucids were overthrown by the Parthians there was a slow renewal of the Zoroastrian infrastructure and the texts were increasingly written down.

The full canon of twenty-one sections or Nasks of the Zoroastrian holy books was written down and established in the time of the succeeding Sasanian Empire, after 224 CE. It was only around this time that Zoroastrianism became the official state religion of the empire, led by the high priest Tansar and his successor Kadir. The Avestan alphabet was fully developed and the texts were committed to writing. The language of the people was by this time Middle Persian, or Pahlavi. Older texts were translated into this language and original works were composed in it. The clerical leaders attempted to drive out other religions and to enforce an orthodox standard against which "heretics" would be measured. This trend is obviously not in the true spirit of Zarathustra. For almost two thousand years the Good Religion had flourished without coercion. The time of the Sasanian Empire was a golden age of Persian culture, but one which contained the seeds of its own destruction.

In 636-651 disaster struck again when invading Arabs conquered the Sasanian Empire, bringing the new religion of Islam with them. In the initial onslaught many of the Arab conquerors destroyed Zoroastrian properties and slaughtered thousands of priests, just as Alexander had done. But this time, the Persians were able to have almost immediate and decisive impact on the new intellectual order, in contrast to what the Greeks were able to do to them eight hundred years earlier. Zoroastrianism continued to be practiced and held many of the people together. Arabic replaced Pahlavi as the language of state around 700 CE. But at the same time Pahlavi religious texts continued to be written and recorded right up through the eighth century. Some Pahlavi texts were also even translated into Arabic.

Islam continued to spread in Iran due to the methods of conversion used by the Muslims. In 750 an 'Abbasid Caliphate was established ruling Iran from the capital of Bagdad, a Persian word meaning "Gift of God." Around 900 CE persecution of non-Muslims intensified. A group of Zoroastrians gathered in Khorasan and set out to immigrate to India. It took them many years of hardship to make the journey. They finally arrived on the Indian coast in 936. There they settled along the coast north of Bombay (Mombai). Generally the Parsees, which the Zoroastrians in India came to be called, prospered in India. Only episodes when Muslims actually came to power in the province of Gujurat did they have hardships. The Parsees could not engage in attempts to convert the local population as a condition of peaceful relations with them. Back in Iran periods of persecution alternated with times of relative tolerance for the next few centuries.

Religious knowledge and zeal waned among the Parsees over the centuries, and those in Iran became more and more isolated. Nevertheless, the Iranian priesthood sent letters of instruction (*rivayats*) to the brethren living in India. The Parsees in India got a stroke of good luck when the British acquired Bombay as their commercial hub in 1661. Parsees moved there in droves and prospered in cooperation with the British. They began to build fire-temples and develop a Western-style educational system.

Back in Iran the 1700s and the 1800s were times of harsh persecutions. The Parsees of India continued to prosper and they turned their attention to the plight of the Iranis and formed societies to help and aid them. Meanwhile, the Parsees were also open to reforms and influences from the West, as well as from the Hindu majority which surrounded them in India.

The Present Situation

Today Zoroastrians remain a small minority in the land of their origin. Muslim authorities over the centuries have often allowed the survivors to continue their faith, as they are said to have been given this favor by Mohammed himself.

The fact that some Zoroastrians survive in Iran today, and that some of their fire-temples continue to exist, and that the ancient signs and symbols of past Zoroastrian glory continue to be used, is a testimony both to the nationalistic fervor of the Iranians and to their deep-level and ancient tradition of tolerance. If the reader is astounded by this statement, and is thinking of the excesses of intolerance now being practiced by the Shi'ite Muslim government of the Islamic Republic of Iran, I would only contrast the history of that country with what the Christians did in Europe. No vestige of the pre-Christian religions in Europe were allowed to survive, no minority of people still worshipping the old gods exist, no ancient temples of the native gods continue to function. The key to the survival of the Zoroastrians in Iran probably lies in Iranian nationalism. The Zoroastrians remain as living reminders of the glories of Iran's past, when it was not just one more Islamic country, but the fountainhead of wisdom to the world and the center of the world's greatest empire.

At present there are no more than 300,000 Zoroastrians in the world. They live in Iran and India— mostly around the city of Bombay. However, many have immigrated to the United Kingdom and to the United States. In America they are mostly concentrated in the major metropolitan areas.

History, as we have seen, made it necessary for the Zoroastrians to evolve into an ethnic group. In Iran the Muslims hemmed them in, while in India, as a way of getting along with the Hindu majority, the Parsees also developed into an ethnically isolated community. The Hindus welcomed the Parsees as long as they did not try to convert Hindus. Hinduism is an ancestral religion, and a direct continuation of the kind of religion originally practiced by the Indo-Iranians. To subject a Hindu family member to conversion to another faith would also erode the family unit. Thus the Parsees evolved back into a kind of ethnic model very much akin to the one practiced by their host Hindus. For all of these reason Zoroastrians eventually adopted the idea that they would not seek, nor would they accept, conversions to their faith. In general this is the situation we find today.

This general non-conversion policy is probably a wise one. The present-day Zoroastrians, whether in Iran, India or in the West, are the product of a millennia-long history. Their achievements of surviving and actually thriving under these conditions are heroic efforts that should be honored by us today. They have acquired a complex cultural texture of traditions and practices which we in the West have generally lost. But we cannot just step into their stream of culture. For example, it is forbidden for non-Parsees to enter the fire-temples in India. The presence of non-Zoroastrians would disrupt the sacrality of the place. We of the Occidental Branch do not want to disturb the traditions or practices of our eastern brethren. One could only imagine what an influx of Westerners into the system would do to their social matrix. Rather we wish to take our inspiration directly from the Truth of the Wise Lord and with the insightful guidance of the eastern brethren develop, with the Grace of Ahura Mazda, our own branch of the tree. We wish to support the old Zoroastrian school and educate the general population about its existence and teachings, as well as encourage those born into the Zoroastrian faith to realize what a gift it is to be part of such a glorious and important tradition. But our own religious traditions must be rooted in our own culture and in our own history, things which developed apart from the cultural streams that shaped the eastern realm. The light that now dawns in the West is the newest oldest religion in the world— the disciplined utilization of wisdom provided by the light of insight.

Chapter 4
The Need for the Good Religion in the West

Here we want to explore why the good Religion is needed in our society today, and why it is needed now. Most everyone today feels a certain sense of crisis in life and culture. Something is fundamentally wrong with the world, and it feels like it is all leading up to something. Largely these are feelings that every generation has had, especially after the establishment of Christian churches in the West had instilled a sense of apocalyptic urgency. This was instilled for reasons of coercion and manipulation through fear, and it plays into universal human psychology as each of us approaches our own mortality. Through the centuries there have always been crises and moments of great historical drama— the early part of the twentieth century, for example. We are not living in such a time. Our time is far more frightening. We see the world not heading toward a great explosive event, but toward a long, boring and stultifying sleep. Our crises are born of a lack of real activity, not an overabundance of it. We feel increasingly imprisoned by overbearing authority as our opportunities for the pursuit of happiness (*ushta*) are progressively strangled off.

In this environment there is a need for some sort of revolutionary change. Something has to change, or nothing will change. The first change has to come from within the individual. Individuals must practice Good Thoughts (*humata*), and must of necessity speak Good Words (*hukhta*) and these must lead to Good Deeds (*khwarshta*). If this train of action is followed to its individual end, it will by necessity involve the banding together of others of like mind and spirit. Individual transformation linked directly to social interaction with others undergoing the same transformation inevitably leads to cultural change and transformation. Change for the sake of change has no merit, only change for the sake of the Good has any value.

Most people are fooled into believing that our crises are "political" and they get caught up in believing that they will be saved by some politician or some political party. This is smoke and mirrors born in the House of Lies. Our problems are not "political," but rather *cultural*. Making laws, policies and programs will not solve anything— as should be clear from the self-evident fact that they have never solved anything in the past. They usually only make the problems worse in a self-perpetuating web work of Lies. Our problems can be traced to cultural degeneration, which does result in an increased belief in Lies, which leads to placing ourselves at the mercy of policy makers with a vested interest in making the problems worse resulting in the Liars convincing the mass of people that more such policies are necessary to get us out of trouble. Really the only way out is cultural regeneration through a recognition of the Truth.

As our culture has degenerated over the course of the last millennium so too has our physical environment. The Good Religion sees the natural world as a direct reflection of the spiritual world. Things that affect the spiritual world have repercussions in the physical one, but the reverse is equally true. Just as Good Deeds are seen as superior to Good Words or Thoughts (because the Deeds include the Thoughts and Words as well), the physical environment of our planet will eventually be in a way superior to heaven. It is to be the final manifestation of the heavenly realm in eternal and perfected form at the time of the "Making Wonderful." Humanity is responsible for maintaining and regenerating the physical environment as a duty to the Good Religion itself. Those who would wish to improve the environment have no better theories than the Mazdan ideas on this subject with which to support their desires. Ultimately the atheist can always say: "So what?' and the Christian can say: "The Lord is coming soon, and the world will be destroyed and judged by him, so who cares?" In the Good Religion we want to preserve the world and perfect it, as the Wise Lord has taught us to strive for. Humanity has an active role in this.

Our present world is beset by a general atmosphere of crisis. People want and need "change." But just because you are miserable in your present state does not mean that it is wise to create changes for the mere sake of making changes in the "hope" that everything will get better. False change is no solution. The patterns of positive transformation are well-known, they are also known to be difficult, often painful, and sometimes dangerous. The Good Religion teaches these methods. The keys to true magic are at home with those who invented it: the Magians. The aim of the Good Religion, the Magian Way, is happiness, *ushta*, which synthesizes wisdom, strength and well-being. These are the guidelines needed by modern man, as they are needed by humanity at all stages of time and in all historical contexts. The crisis cannot be avoided by adopting defensive stances and lurching from one critical situation to the next— a clear and straightforward attack on the source of all crisis is called for. Forces of destruction, chaos, disease and ignorance must be confronted and defeated with the powerful weapons provided by the rituals and ethics of the Good Religion.

What one finds when this is done is that *development* takes place. By development (rather than "change") we mean that there is an unfolding of our own inner, divine, natures. As each stage of the unfoldment occurs, we move from one *form* to another, and are thus trans*form*ed. Revolutionary alterations in our forms of life, using imagined and never-before-seen patterns, lead to disaster. Such shadowy and dreamy notions are the whisperings of the Lie. The

34

twentieth century was littered with their results and the new century shows no present signs of cultural improvement. The West needs renovation and the Good Religion can show the way.

Current trends in Western religion are disturbing to many. In Western Europe church attendance is minimal and belief has been waning in the face of decrepit institutions devoid of spirituality, whether Protestant or Catholic. In America atheism is probably the fastest growing "religion." "New Age" teachings and alternative spiritualities are attractive at first, but more often than not lose their "charm" with individuals after a few years. People either turn to another "alternative," return to some conventional church, or give up on religion altogether. The reason for all this is that the conventional denominations are spiritually bankrupt— preachers have to be entertainers to keep the flock in the pews. The New Age failure is due to the lack of traditional depth most of these entities have, as well as their often anti-social orientation. "New spiritualities" tend to separate the believers from the larger social environment. This leads to a sense of alienation over time.

The Good Religion answers these concerns. Because it is the most ancient form of true religion, and because it has touched, if not fundamentally created, many of the world's so-called Great Religions, it has both traditional depth and deep-level connectivity. It connects us not only with our own deep-level (pre-Christian) roots, but also to our historical religions, be they Christian, Jewish or Muslim. The religion has been carried forth in a traditional manner from the time of Zarathustra, with rites and prayers that were created in those days which continue to be performed today just as they were almost four-thousand years ago. No other religion can make similar claims. The Occidental Temple has much pioneering work to do to bring the essence of this vision for the first time in an undefiled way to the West. Again we see the wonderful blend of tradition and innovation as a necessity. Innovation is necessary to renovation.

So-called Western Civilization is in trouble, it is in crisis mode, it requires the recognition that the problems are radical, deep-level cultural ones, not political or economic ones. Asking a politician to fix our problems is like asking a dermatologist to cure the cancerous tumor that has just erupted on the surface of a person's skin. In the form of Mazdaism we have a formula that worked in the past for the generation of great cultures in which the virtues we honor today were practiced and exercised. A study of the Parsees of India show how adaptable Zoroastrian ideas are to the modern world. They do not merely survive here, they are thriving where they still exist. Mazdan ideas and practices stem from common Indo-European roots and are therefore not to be seen as "exotic" in the fundamental sense. The root principles are shared by all Indo-European peoples from Ireland to India and Iran,

The West will be renewed with a fresh look at its own deepest-level roots. Much of the imagery and symbolism used takes advantage of the exotic allure of the East. The utility of this is that it supplies the freshness needed to make the impact required. Also, we have found that the actual *sounds* of the Avestan prayers, or *mathras*, have their own power that goes beyond their literal meanings. The West needs this message, and it comes at the time predicted, at the beginning of a new millennium. Here in the darkest hour we glimpse the first sparks of the Making Wonderful.

IDEOLOGICAL

Chapter 5
Theology

The Good Religion is monotheistic. There is only one God. This God is absolute consciousness, or Wisdom, focused and eternal. This God is so abstract, however, that there must be entities which the Wise Lord creates in order to work his will in the cosmos. The first and foremost of these are the Bounteous Immortals, the Amesha Spentas. Beyond these there exist a great number of angels, or *yazatas* (those worthy of worship) which help fulfill the divine will, and at the same time aid humanity in all manner of ways.

The present-day follower of the Good Religion in the West needs to be familiar with these entities as a matter of inner, spiritual knowledge. None of these are believed in in a "fundamentalist" way. They are not thought of as creatures floating around in the sky. They are deeper and more pervasive forces than that. Mythic imagery gives initial handles, but the names of the beings often give the key to the philosophical and inner meaning of the concept in question.

The Good Religion always borders on philosophy. As we have seen historically the ideas of Zarathustra were taken up by the Greeks who shaped an independent system of philosophy, "love of wisdom," on them. Within the Good Religion myth, ritual, science and philosophy all happily mix together in a harmonious whole. Philosophy naturally emerges from theology as abstraction is the work of the Good Mind.

Ahura Mazda

Zarathustra conceived of the unity of God. This one God, from which all the other gods and goddesses are derived, is pure, focused consciousness. Zarathustra coined the descriptive name for this concept as Ahura Mazda, literally "Lord Wisdom." So the Prophet saw not only the unity of God, but also the character of this God as being *consciousness*. The other gods and goddesses with which he was familiar were then seen as abstract concepts. He renamed them for their functions, and saw them as extension of the one divine will. They became his *messengers*.

Although the phrase *Ahura Mazda* is masculine in a grammatical sense, the concept behind the name is beyond the duality of gender. Ahura Mazda bears very few, if any, anthropomorphic characteristics. This is a far cry from the highly humanized Jehovah, who is masculine, angry, loving, fearful, jealous, and all the other things any other ancient storm god might demonstrate. The "personality" of the Wise Lord is only expressed through the many aspects expressed by the Bounteous Immortals and the numerous angels (*yazatas*).

The Wise Lord existed before anything else, this is the First Principle, and he is eternal. He is the the Creator of all that is Good—this includes the material universe and mankind. As the focus of Wisdom he is all-seeing: he knows the past, present and future of everything. There is nothing more powerful in the universe than the Wise Lord. As we will see later, this does not mean that he is *all*-powerful. The genius of God is that he has created humanity to act as his agents in the material universe. Good people help him grow in power. Humanity is — or can be — the engine of God. He sees humans as his partners in creation and as his friends and family. We will see how this is so later.

Ahura Mazda is motivated by perfecting his Creation and defeating the forces of evil — ignorance, chaos, lies, death — in the cosmos. Everything he enacts is dedicated to this purpose. The Lord acts through extensions, which are called the Bounteous Immortals, or Amesha Spentas (archangels) as well as *yazatas* (angels).

Diagram of Amesha Spentas in Conjunction with the Human Soul

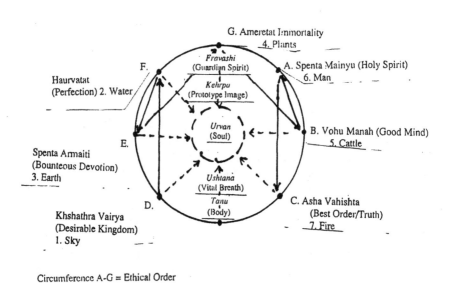

Circumference A-G = Ethical Order
Lines   1-7 = Creation Order
Broken Lines   = Inputs to the Soul

40

Amesha Spentas

There are seven Bounteous Immortals arrayed around the Wise Lord. Each one protects and promotes one of the Lord's Seven Creations. With these Archangels, as they have sometimes been called, we can see how the Wise Lord begins to interact productively with his Creation in all of its constituent parts. We are reminded of the meaning of each of these entities through their places in the sacred calendar as months and certain days are dedicated to them for our instruction and attention.

In what follows we will see the characteristics of each of the Amesha Spentas and most importantly take a look at the actual tasks that humanity is charged with enacting, inwardly and outwardly, to do the work of the Wise Lord through these Bounteous Ones.

Spenta Mainyu

Spenta Mainyu means "Bounteous Spirit," or "Holy Spirit." This is Mazda's active, creative and motivating force in the cosmos. He is the protector and patron of humanity. It is the work of the individual Mazdan to learn to integrate the spiritual and physical realms. When this is done he or she can begin to recognize the essence of divinity.

Vohu Manah

The name Vohu Manah literally means "the Good Mind." It is the Good Mind which Zarathustra so fervently sought and received. It makes man be able to understand things intellectually so that he can discriminate between the good and the bad and choose correctly. This is the protector of cattle, by which is understood all beneficial animals. Under the tutelage of the Good Mind man must learn to recognize the ethical aspects of life. Those who have done this will naturally begin to care for the animals and the natural environment in all dimensions.

Asha Vahishta

The Avestan word *asha* is one of the most complex to understand. Its meaning embodies the concepts of *truth* and *order*. This is the Sanskrit *rita*. Right order/truth is of paramount importance in the Good Religion. The name Asha Vahishta literally means "the *Best* Truth/Order." This takes it beyond the merely Good into the superlative realm of the the *Best*. Some translators use the term "Righteousness" for this concept, but that seems too loaded with unintended connotations. *Asha* is the Order which is Truth. Asha Vahishta regulates things on a physical, psychological and spiritual level in humanity. It is the protector of the ritual fire (*Atar*). The individual must learn to recognize and absorb *Asha* in order to bring about harmony and happiness (*ushta*) in life. This is the *asha* of pure and undefiled wisdom symbolized by the ritual fire.

Khshathra Vairya

Here the name is translated as "Desirable and Sovereign Kingdom." This Archangel fills the ancient function of sovereignty— the ability to exercise independent power. This power is good in an of itself, but can be misused by bad people. Hence the Good Religion focuses on the idea of the Desirable Kingdom, a sovereign kingdom which is desired by the people and which is in harmony with the divine and public will. It represents the power of the Kingdom of God. The sky and metals are under the protection of Khshathra Vairya. It is the individual's task to accumulate this power and to exercise it from within the Kingdom of God which is within the personal sphere, and thus do so with discrimination between what is the best and worst.

Spenta Armaiti

Here the name means Bounteous Piety or Devotion. This is a pattern by which the ability of the Wise Lord's creations to receive benefits is maintained. The Wise Lord is constantly giving, but often his creations are put in circumstances — or they put themselves in circumstancess — where the benefits cannot be properly received; Spenta Armaiti keeps this channel open. This archangel is the protector of the Earth. Man is to show devotion to the environment and learn to be virtuous, sensitive and just.

Haurvatat

The meaning of the name is Health and Well-Being. This is the completeness and perfection of God's presence in the world. Haurvatat protects the waters of the world. Mankind is charged with the responsibility of perfecting and completing God's creation in the world so that evil is pushed out and we move closer to the perfected state of the world.

Ameretat

This name means Immortality. Undyingness is bestowed on elements in God's creation in order to ensure the continuity of well-being and the essence of the Creation itself. Ameretat protects the plant world of the planet. The human task is to work toward the realization of continuity in both the corporeal and spiritual worlds. In doing this man works toward the eventual Making Wonderful when the whole of Creation will reach a state of happiness.

Yazatas or Angels

The functions of the seven Amesha Spentas are clearly derived from the most ancient Aryan theological structure. Zarathustra saw through the structure and was enlightened on a divine level by the Good Mind (Vohu Manah) to the inner secrets of what had before been simple belief. Subsequent generations of priests in the school he established in his lifetime analyzed many other mythological figures and a system of *yazatas* (ones worthy of worship) arose. These are the origin of the doctrine of angels in other religions. There are dozens of such entities in the eastern branch of Zoroastrianism. We supplement these with some of our own from the West in the Occidental Temple of the Wise Lord. However, here is not the place to go into these ideas.

In the eastern Zoroastrian calendars each day of the month is dedicated to one of either the Wise Lord himself, to one of the Amesha Spentas or to one of the major yazatas.

It is universally accepted that the idea of angels found in Judaism, Christianity and Islam was derived from Zoroastrian doctrines concerning the Amesha Spentas and *yazatas*. The word "angel" comes from the Greek *angelos*, "messenger." Angels are extensions of divine will, they are parts of God himself. This doctrine is clear and logical in the Good Religion. The idea is misunderstood and illogical as expressed by Christian churchmen when they say that Satan was an "angel" who "rebelled" against God. This again introduces confusion and unreason to their system. Angels do not have free will, therefore they by definition cannot rebel. Any demonic entities must by definition have an origin outside and independent of God. Here, as elsewhere, the Mazdan answer is logical.

We do not have the space here to discuss the twenty-six or so major *yazatas* in any detail. But we can describe some of them and the deep-level roots out of which they were recognized by *magavans*, or enlightened initiates, in possession of Good Minds.

One group of *yazatas* is directly derived from the old Aryan gods. Here too the most ancient mythic ideology of tripartition is present. We find:

I. Mithra is the *yazata* of the contract, truth, light and all-creatures. He is the old god who was once paired with the Lord of Wisdom in the ancient Indo-European tripartite system. He answers to Týr in Norse mythology. Mithra is certainly the second most important entity in the Zoroastrian "pantheon." He is widely depicted in Zoroastrian art with a halo and shaking the hands of those whom he befriends. Mithra also continued to be worshipped in cults separate from orthodox Zoroastrianism and was important in the Hellenized system during the Seleucid Empire. In a way Mithra is the foreign ambassador of the Wise Lord to the world.

II. Verathraghna is the *yazata* of overcoming of any resistance and victory. He is the heroic dragon slayer and has taken the place of the demonized Indara (Vedic Indra) who was the god of the over-indulgers. Verathraghna expresses physical power, to be sure, but also the spiritual power of the will to overcome obstacles in life.

III. Anahita is a feminine *yazata* who kept her name from ancient times. She is the "spotless" perfect one. She is the yazata of fertility, power and beauty. She remained a personal favorite of Zarathustra. Another *yazata* who belongs to this class is Airyaman. His name is related to that of "Aryan," and indicates that he rules over health, fellowship and friendship. His meaning was one of tribal solidarity in the old, pre-Zarathustrian system, but he is universalized to mean all those who follow the Good Religion are sponsored by his friendship. His name is cognate to the Germanic *Irmin-*.

Another group comes from a set of important celestial bodies. But the objects themselves are seen as visible manifestations of more abstract realities as well. This is true of almost all visible things. The entities are: Hvar Khshaeta, the radiant sun (imperishable, cleansing); Mah, the moon (thoughtfulness and prosperity); Tishtrya, the star Sirius (giver of rains and router of drought). This complex of Sun-Moon-Star(s) is an important symbolic triad.

A large group of *yazatas* is connected with natural phenomena of the earth in one way or another. The Earth herself is represented by Zam who is her protector. Vata is the *yazata* of the Good Wind, while Asman is the Stone which is the vault of heaven and the container of the other creations. Most importantly there is Atar, that is Fire. As we will see in the cosmological chapter, terrestrial fire is a true symbol of the Divine Mind. When we say *symbol* we mean that it is a tangible manifestation of the essence of something beyond the phenomenon itself. It is a *part* of a greater whole.

In orthodox Zoroastrianism by far the greatest number of *yazatas* are clearly connected to abstract or ritualistic concepts. Khwarena is Divine Grace sometimes visible as a "halo." (The use of the radiant spiritual light shining from behind a god's head or shoulders is originally a part of Zoroastrian art.) Daena is a feminine *yazata* who is Insight and Conscience. We will meet her again when we address the soul and what happens after death. Sraosh is Obedience and Discipline which is necessary in the correct performance of prayers and rituals. Rashnu is Judgment, Raman is Joy and Peace, Chista is the One who Teaches. Specifically connected to ritual activities are the *yazatas* Mathra Spenta, the Holy Word (spoken ritual formulas) and Haoma the *yazata* exemplifying the sacred drink used in ritual of the Good Religion. Zarathustra spoke out heavily against the over-indulgence in *haoma* and over-sacrificing of animals being done by the warrior-class in his world. The *haoma*, used in moderation and under the right circumstances brings the mind to its peak performance.

One *yazata* is named for a single animal, Geush, the cow or ox. This animal stands for *all* good animals, by which we mean all animals that are innocent and are of benefit to humans or other animals. She is righteous, courageous and nourishing. (Evil creatures of Ahriman are those which only harm others and are of no use to the world, for example scorpions and fire-ants.)

Demonology
Ahriman and His Minions

As we will see in the chapter on the origin and organization of the cosmos, the Good Religion has a whole doctrine of entities which oppose Ahura Mazda and the beneficial entities. In the ancient terminology these are called *daevas*. It is unnecessary to study anything about these entities. We only need to know how to oppose and defeat them in our lives and in the world. They have none of the charm and heroic rebelliousness of Western Devils. Milton and the Romantics made a hero of the Judeo-Christian Satan, and figures such as Satan, or Lucifer can be identified as conduits for the introduction of wisdom and knowledge in Western mythology. Jesus said: "Let them be as wise as serpents." But there is no such Romanticism in the system of the Good Religion. Ahriman and his minions are cruel, ignorant, stupid forces of pure destruction and chaos with no redeeming value whatsoever. Anyone who would "worship" Ahriman is a fool. Dealing with these devils can only bring misery, death and deception. Their patterns of behavior lead humanity into bad thoughts, bad words and bad deeds. Another way of saying this is that destructive thoughts, words and actions, are things that trend in the opposite direction from that which any sane person would *consciously* choose to go. These entities express either an excess or deficiency in everything they do. Water is good, but a devil will drown you in it, when he is not causing you to die of thirst.

In some Iranian systems outside of orthodox Zoroastrianism, for example Mithraism, we see that Ahriman might have been placated, propitiated or "bought off," to try to avoid the negative impact of his activities. In ancient times this was also done among various populations in the Mediterranean region with regard to Jehovah who was widely "feared" even by non-Jews for the destruction and misery he could cause to those who did not give him his "due." It was from among these many non-Jewish "god-fearers" that many early Christian converts came, and it is due to this that the early church moved away from its Zoroastrian roots.

It is relatively pointless to go into the complexities of Zoroastrian demonology. The point is to combat their powers. This is done with the universal weapons: *Humata-Hukhta-Khvarshta*: Good Thoughts, Good Words and Good Deeds. These we will discuss in detail later. But to get a feel for the nature of the archdemons as posited by the Good Religion we need only hear their names and read what they do:

Ahriman: Evil Spirit— Destroys Man
Akoman: Evil Mind— Destroys Animals
Andar: Untruth and Disorder— Pollutes the Fire
Savul: Undesirable Kingdom— Pollutes the Sky
Taromat: Impiety— Pollutes the Earth
Tarich: Imperfection— Pollutes the Waters
Zairich: Mortality— Destroys the Plants

As is apparent these "demons" are names for processes and events which occur contrary to the direction of development desired by the Good Mind, the Truth and the Wise Lord. This is far from the puerile demonology of those who were inspired by this system in antiquity and who understood it only partially. The fact that bad things exist is logically proof of the existence of forces and patterns which cause them. The daevas are not so much personal entities with individual wills and conscious plans, rather they are unthinking patterns and structures which parasitically infest and infect everything they come into contact with— if they are able. These cannot be ascribed to the Good God, therefore they originate and are identical with Ahriman and his minions. It helps to give a name to the opposition so we can better understand what we must eliminate.

Overall the *daevas*, or demons, are guided by the Druj, the Lie in opposition to Asha, the Truth. The Lie constantly tells Man that he is no good, stupid, cannot help himself, is doomed to death and destruction, that man belongs to the daevas, and that cruel thoughts, deceitful words and trickery are pathways to happiness. All this is a pack of lies.

It should be said that very few of the old pagan Iranian gods were permanently demonized in the Good Religion. They were for the most part reinterpreted and understood in more philosophized forms. This is very different from the way medieval churchmen demonized the old gods and goddesses of Europe. The people in Europe, as in Iran, did not want to give up their native gods and goddesses entirely. In Iran they were allowed back into the system under new conditions, whereas in Europe those who wished to continue to follow the old ways had to do so either by infusing old meanings into new Christian imagery, or actually sympathize with the Devil of the new religion.

In general we find that in the Good Religion philosophy cannot be separated from theology. This is because the reform of Zarathustra meant that the Good (= Powerful) Mind could directly perceive abstract principles, just as the gods and goddesses were thought to be able to do. The theology of the Good Religion mandates that the individual become a philosopher— a direct "lover of wisdom." Wisdom loves us, so too must we love Wisdom. We will address philosophical issues more precisely in chapter eight.

Chapter 6
Cosmology

In order to understand the philosophy underlying the Good Religion we have to understand the shape and origin of the cosmos as well as that of humanity. We have to understand what the world is, and what man's place and role is in it. These are, after all, the questions that have occupied the human mind: where am I, who am I, and what am I doing here? The Good Religion has profound and optimistic answers to these questions. Here we will examine the first of these questions: Where are we? What is the universe and how did it come about?

In our tradition the most informative sources on these questions are contained in two versions of one work, the *Bundahishn*, which has a longer and shorter edition. This material is in accord with what we glimpse from the Avestan sources as well. In the beginning the Wise Lord existed within his realm of Endless Light and he is and was eternal, conscious, infinite and totally good. At the edge of this realm was a station of shadow or darkness where the entity called Ahriman evolved, characterized by "after-wit" (ignorance) and a desire for destruction. There was a great void between these two. The realm of Ahura Mazda was in a perfect spiritual state (*menog*). The Wise Lord, because of his omniscient wisdom, knew that Ahriman would eventually attack his realm. This was only logical since Ahriman was by his very nature ignorant and destructive.

Ahriman burst through the defenses of *menog* and began to attack and pollute the realm, but the Wise Lord pushed him back and frightened him into retreat. The mixture of the good and evil states had begun. Ahriman returned to his realm where he began to fabricate a legion of destructive creatures with which to attack the Light. The Wise Lord knew of Ahriman's plan and as an act of mercy offered him peace, if Ahriman would refrain from attack. The Wise Lord knew that he would eventually defeat Ahriman, but a war would cause great suffering. Ahriman, in his typical ignorance and desire for destruction, rejected the offer.

Ahura Mazda then chanted the *mathra* known as *Ahunvar* (*Yatha ahu vairyo...*) which put Ahriman and his creations into a state of stupefaction for an age during which the Wise Lord created the good physical universe in preparation for the future war with the forces of destruction. The Wise Lord also ordained that there would be three Ages or "times" of the cosmos, the first period when Good and Evil were unmixed, the second a time of mixture and conflict between Good and Evil (the Age in which we now find ourselves) and the future state of the victory of Good over Evil.

In the creative process the Wise Lord first created the six Amesha Spentas, whom we met in the previous chapter. They are ordered in two different ways: the ethical order, which shows how they were created in *menog*, and then a creation order as to how they were manifested in the material world (*getig*). They were first created in the following order:

1. Holy Spirit
2. Good Mind
3. Truth
4. Desirable Kingdom
5. Devotion
6. Perfection
7. Immortality

Then the Wise Lord sent these out to shape the framework of the material universe as a bulwark against the onslaught of Ahriman. In this creative process the Amesha Spentas were implemented in the following order:

1. Sky: Desirable Kingdom
2. Water: Perfection
3. Earth: Devotion:
4. Plants: Immortality
5. Cattle (Animals): Good Mind
6. Man: Holy Spirit
7. Fire: Truth

As realms in which these entities existed before they became manifest the Wise Lord shaped seven circular spheres of the cosmic order, called *karshvars*, emanated from the Wise Lord. These are reflected in our world as various regions of the planet, but have their origin in the arrangement of the seven fiery spheres above. The origin of the word *karshvar-* indicates that it meant a "circular-land" and clearly initially were cosmological zones or spheres reflected in the organization of this planet.

These emanations are both spiritual and physical at the same time. This is the essence of Mazdan science and spirituality. It is diametrically opposed to the duality as misunderstood in many religious viewpoints which only poorly grasped the system of Zarathustra. Other systems slide off into a spirit:matter duality. Zarathustra and his followers taught that Mazda and his emanations are multivalent, having spiritual properties, but also manifesting in their natures a material aspect. The duality inherent in the teachings of Zarathustra involves the dichotomy between good and evil as *moral* values. Negative moral values exist, and they too have physical manifestations. One cosmological text recounts:

> And from this he brought forth the whole creation into existence. And when it had been brought into existence, he bore it in his body. And he kept increasing in size and everything got better and better, and then he created them, one after the other out of his own body.
>
> And first he created the sky from his head...
> And he created the earth from his feet...
> And he created the water from his tears...
> And he created the plants from his hair...
> And he created the fire from his mind...

This is a Mazdan conception which holds that the original Man is the active agent in the creation of the world, rather than as a victim of a sacrifice. This text shows clear correspondence to the most archaic Indo-European pattern of the parts of the cosmos being created out of parts of the original cosmic Man. It also gives the clear link between *fire* and the *mind* of the divinity. This fire is not just a symbol of the mind of God, it is a physical manifestation of its spiritual nature. As such the Magians were never "fire worshippers," but rather those who worship (i.e., give honor to) the mind of God, of the Wise Lord, by being in the presence of a material manifestation of his spiritual reality. Mazdans hold that the fire forms a ritual *gateway* between the mind of the Wise Lord and the other six creations. Being in the presence of the ritual fire can sanctify objects and humans. The proof of this is found in experience of the results of Mazdan practices, not in blind faith toward the concepts.

The idea that divinity created the cosmos out of itself using the abstract power of the mind is a Mazdan revelation— and one that would have far-reaching influence throughout the world.

So in the teachings of the Good Religion we see that the cosmos was created by the Wise Lord in the following order:

1) Sky [space]
2) Water
3) Earth
4) Plants
5) Animals
6) Humans
7) Fire

These are the Seven Creations that are held to be so sacred by all Mazdans and Zoroastrians.

49

There grew a great mountain, Mount Hara (also called Alborz), which was the point of origin for all light as well as all water. The sky was symbolically said to be made of stone or metal. The earth was divided into seven *karshvars* or countries inhabitable by men which was a reflection of the cosmic order in which there are seven regions, but only the central one is that of the earth where humans live. From the seed of the first "man," Gayomart, eventually slain by the evil spirit, Angra Mainyu, sprang the first man and woman in the form of plants. Similarly from the slain bovine sprang the seed of all animals, as well as some plants. But from the Saena Tree which grows at the center of the cosmos sprang the seeds of all plants— most notably those that give wisdom and immortality.

This is not the place to enter into the esoteric details of Mazdan cosmology. These traditional ideas are introduced here to show the idea of the multiple levels or dimensions of reality reflected in and out of the emanations of the Wise Lord. It is obviously an object for further study.

The cosmology contains secrets about how things are brought into being, that is, how things are constructed or created in general. This process is intimately linked to the structure of the human composition, which we will see in the next chapter.

Once the perfect spiritual and material universe was created, it was attacked by Ahriman. At noon on Nowruz Ahriman pierced the sky from above in the form of a serpent and entered the Wise Lord's creation to try to kill and sicken everything in his path. He let loose Greed, Pestilence, Disease, Hunger, Illness and Lethargy on the bodies of Man and Animals. The Cosmic Cow was sickened and died. All Seven Creations were under attack. Man discovered Fire and began to fight back.

The Soul of the Cow prayed to the divine beings of the upper worlds to send a hero, a redeemer to help the world. As an answer to the prayer of the Soul of the Cow Zarathustra was incarnated. His mission was to make humanity aware of the true nature of the world and of mankind itself and additionally to show the way to vanquish Ahriman. A series of similar saviors or teachers were sent subsequently and will be sent in the future in this continuing effort. They are called Saoshyants. Eventually Ahriman will be defeated, will retreat into unconsciousness and inactivity, and will leave the world through the same hole through which he arrived.

Mythic cosmologies are not to be taken literally. They describe in spiritual and eternally true forms how things came into being, and how things come into being in general, how things are organized on an abstract or ideal level, and how things end. In short, mythic cosmology is a spiritual map of the world, the context in which we live and in which we have to operate. It is based on tradition and forms an ideal toward which we are to strive. Purely materialistic science has an ever shifting cosmology, but traditional cosmology is eternally true. One of the main purposes of the study of traditional and esoteric cosmology is to help us understand the magnificence of the cosmos and our own role in it.

Chapter 7
Origin and Structure of the Human Being

The Purpose of Man

Man is one of the Seven Creations of Ahura Mazda. The others are water, earth, plants, animals, the sky (atmosphere) and fire. Each of these creations was brought into being in order to act as a way for the Good to overcome the forces of destruction and chaos. All of these creations are necessary, but fire and man hold special positions. Fire is a reflection of the very mind of God himself, and man is the reflection of God in a *potential* state. Mankind's own struggle for perfection is an act of co-creativity with the deity. As mankind perfects itself under the precepts of the Good Religion (under whatever imperfect or incomplete label) the world is transformed into a more perfect state. This is the meaning and purpose of Man: to act as a warrior for the Wise Lord in his battle against the forces of destruction and disorder.

The human being is not a simple creation. Humans are a complex of various parts, all of which are to work in good order and harmony in order to reach their full potential of power.

In other words, like the other traditional Indo-European views on the composition of human beings, that of ancient Iran was polypsychic, i.e., there were a number of bodies or souls which went together to make up the entire living human being. This archaic pattern has been more or less held intact by present-day Mazdans. The model of the living, healthy and whole person is that person who has all of these parts and in whom these parts work together harmoniously and vigorously. Death is characterized by a shattering of the parts of the whole. As a part of the world's final stage of development, the *Frasho-kereti* ("Making-Wonderful") the shattered parts of the whole will be reunited and the one you originally were and the one who is your ultimate potential finally realized will be made manifest. As the Wise Lord created the material universe as a reflection of the heavenly one there will be no duality in the end. The material and spiritual will become parts of one manifest whole. This is the origin of the idea of the "resurrection of the dead." Many people find the idea of the resurrection of the dead, adopted by Judaism and accepted by Christian orthodoxy as well, an absurd notion, and prefer to believe in an entirely spiritual, incorporeal heaven. The idea of a purely spiritual, non-physical, heavenly realm as the destination of good souls is a purely pagan idea. Zarathustra's philosophical stance on this followed the logic of Ahura Mazda's physical creation being a manifestation of Goodness and as a battlefield for the waging of war against the forces of Ahriman. Logically, if this world is Good, and was created by the Good for the Good, it should in the end be perfected, and all of the Good entities that live in it, or which have ever lived in it, should be remanifested in physical and perfect forms at the conclusion of the process in which the Truth triumphs over the Lie.

A fundamental question posed by all religions — and usually answered by them — What is humanity and what is its purpose? The Judeo-Christian tradition concludes that man is to "love and praise God." The Jews and Muslims emphasize man's obedience to God's laws, while Christians emphasize man's acceptance of Christ and the individual forgiveness of sins, and that all men are born sinners as a result of the disobedience of Adam and Eve.

However, the Good Religion has a quite different answer to the fundamental questions at hand: We hold that humanity was incarnated from spiritual prototypes in *menog* (the spiritual realm) and that all individuals possess a spark of the divine from this; we came here to fight for the Good on the side of the Wise Lord and we are needed by him to complete and perfect his creations and thereby increase his power to overcome the forces of Ahriman. As each individual makes progress in self-perfection, reflected necessarily in that individual's words and deeds, the environment in all phases is increasingly perfected. This is how man aids the Wise Lord and how the battle against the forces of death, disease and destruction is carried forward. Development is desired and promoted. This is why new developments in the tradition, such as the manifestation of the Occidental Temple of the Wise Lord, are perfectly in keeping with the original Zarathustrian vision.

Ancient Iranian mythology tells of the creation of Gayomaretan, the first mortal. This is a cosmic man, and a reflection of the image of Ahura Mazda. Ahriman causes this entity's death but not before its seed was "thoroughly purified by the motion of the light of the sun," it was divided into three parts, two of which are guarded by the Wise Lord's messenger to Mankind, Neryosang, the third part went into the earth and after forty years a plant grew, and from this plant emerged Mashya and Mashyanag, the first mortal man and woman. Light came down from the Wise Lord and entered their souls, breath went into them and the Wise Lord spoke to them: "You are the seed of man, you are the parents of the world, you have been given by Me the best perfect devotion ... think good thoughts, speak good words do good deeds, and do not worship the daevas." Their first thought was to "please each other," their first words were: "Ahura Mazda gave the waters, the earth, the trees, the beneficient animals, the stars, the moon, the sun and all good whose manifestation is from Truth and Right Order." Their first deed was to wash themselves thoroughly.

Soon after this, however, Ahriman attacked them, entered their bodies, souls and minds and corrupted them with false beliefs such as that the evil spirit created the waters, earth, plants and animals. For fifty winters they worshipped the daevas, ate poorly and had no desire for sexual intercourse. This first pair struggled with the beliefs and practices of good and evil, when they followed the good precepts they would have breakthroughs and would eat well and sacrifice to the fire and have intercourse and pleasure. From this their first children were born, but Ahriman caused them to devour their offspring, due the sweetness of the children's flesh. Ahura Mazda took the sweetness away, to help the pair end this evil practice. This allegorical myth is about mankind's struggle with good and evil, the nature of the struggle and how God helps man find the right direction again. Mashya and Mashyanag had to make the good choice at every step along the way, and were constantly being corrupted by negative tendencies, just as we are today. We are not condemned by their choices, but we face the same ones every day ourselves.

This myth recounts one part of the heritage and destiny of humankind. But another, more powerful and heroic one, tells us of our true purpose and meaning in the world. At the time when the Wise Lord was preparing to initiate the great battle with the forces of Ahriman he gathered all of the angelic souls, human prototypes in heaven, and asked them to chose to become flesh and blood in the world in order to engage Ahriman and the daevas in battle. The unanimous roar of consent that went up echoes through the ages still. All humans who are now living, who have lived before and those who have yet to be incarnated, are all in possession of one of these divine sparks, these fravashis. It is for this reason that all humans will eventually reach the perfected state, because they began in that state. Much is made of the fact that the Zoroastrians seem to have invented the idea of "heaven and hell," or a future state of rewards and punishments based upon the deeds of a person in this life, for which that person will be judged in a *post-mortem* state. All of this is true. But whereas other religions make this a permanent and irrevocable state, Zoroastrianism teaches that the punishment phase is one of purification. Mythically this is seen as passing through a sea of molten metal— imagery based on ancient Indo-European "trials by ordeal," as well as the symbolism of the tempering of metals. Humans forget their real origins, natures and purposes due to traumas to the soul and the daevic Lies. But each one will awaken at some point— it is the purpose of the Good Religion to teach the Truth and hasten the time of perfection.

55

As we have learned, the ancient peoples knew of a very complex form of psychology and physiology. Because they looked inward so much, they came to know and understand their inner worlds far better than we generally do today. This is why they had so many terms for the various parts that make up the whole human being. The average person only poorly understands what is really meant by "soul," "mind" and "spirit" today. But in ancient times people seem to have had a deep awareness of the soul and its workings. This was true of our own direct ancestors, such as the ancient Celts and Germanic peoples, and equally so of the Indo-Iranians.

From the earliest times we have records talking about forms of the following body-mind concepts:

ahu: This is the essence of life, the life-force. It is your vital existence and the power or energy that holds all of the parts of the individual together in a whole— and which with work can become a harmonious whole.

manah: This is the faculty of pure intellect, consciousness or the mind. It is subject to negative as well as positive influences, harmful or beneficial forms.

urvan: Here we find the soul as such. It is the central spiritual essence of man and is endowed with the faculties of wisdom, reason, intellect, will, knowledge and conscience. It has no location in the body but is rather diffused throughout the entire physical being. It reunites with its *fravashi* after death.

daena: This originally means "insight," which is the idea underlying Iranian religion. It is visualized as a beautiful fifteen-year-old female who will meet the individual at the foot of the Chinvat Bridge. She will be accompanied by a group of dogs. The dogs help drive any evil away, while she, as an embodiment of all of your deeds, good and bad, will "judge" your soul. She is with you always, but may only become visible after death. In Modern Persian this is *dīn*, which was also borrowed into Arabic as a word meaning "religion."

badah: Here we have the part of the soul which constitutes perception (originally through the sense of smell), through and by which we acquire knowledge. This is an innate, inborn wisdom which unfolds during the course of life.

ushi: This originally meant "ear," hence "hearing," from which developed the idea of the power to conceive of things, to construct new things and ideas from within by means of the power of imagination. This is the seat of understanding and the power to conceptualize.

The next two parts go together to form the individual person with the unique personality incarnated in one's present life.

kehrp: This is the the body, shape and image. It is not "physical" in the normal scientific sense, but is the gateway between the spiritual and physical parts of the individual.

tanu: Here we have the individual physical body as present in this incarnation of the soul from the realm of *menog*. It is necessary to the physical presence of the individual self or person.

The physical being is seen as a garment and weapon of the soul. Appended to this body of material is that surrounding the *fravashi* or *farvarti*. The term is derived from a root meaning either "protection" (**fra-vṛti*) or "to chose" (*var-*). This entity shares many aspects with the Germanic *valkyrja* and *fylgja*. The *fravashi* is an ancestral protective spirit or angel, and also the "higher, spiritual self of individuals. Just such *fravashis* actually receive cultic sacrifice" (*Yashts* 26 and 13). But the *fravashis* are not just ancestral spirits, but rather also the pre-existing heavenly entities which act as protective angels for all individuals and as such they have a *warrior*-function. *Fravashis* are visualized as spear-carrying riders who protect and defend heaven. They are called "guardian angels" and indeed this Mazdan lore is the origin of that idea in Western religions.

Also appended to every individual is a *khwarr*. This is the God-given glory or grace, visible on occasion to some as a nimbus around the head and shoulders. The *khwarr* is a storehouse of God-given talents and abilities in latent form. It is up to the individual to develop these. Concerning the *khwarr* and the *urvan* and how they work together, K. P. Mistree writes: "The soul is the motivating force and the prime mover within man while the *khwarr* has within it potential talents which are to be realized by man who must endeavor to nurture and cultivate the *khwarr* to its full capacity, because 'growth, fulfillment and prosperity' are integral parts of Zoroastrian doctrine." (p. 43) R. C. Zaehner called the Good Religion one of "creative evolution." He went on to say that "Man distinguishes himself from the beasts in that he is not merely a product of nature (*chihr*), he has also a moral dimension in that he is possessed of intellect and will (*akhw*)." See Zaehner, 1961, p. 268.

Current esoteric Parsi anthropology (see Mehta, *Our Heritage*, p. 69ff.) outlines the following system. The human being is seen to be made up of nine parts:

Physical

Tanu: the bony structure of the physical body which gives it shape.

Gaitha: all the material internal parts of the body.

Azde: the liquid body, not all of which is visible to the material eye.

<u>Etheric Parts</u>
(die with the physical body)

Keherp: allows perceptions to pass from the spiritual to the material worlds.

Tevishi: sensory vehicle for the transmission of emotions and wishes.

Ushtand: inner life-power which holds the physical and spiritual parts of the person together.

<u>Divine Parts</u>
(immortal)

Urvan: the soul.

Baodhanch: inner inborn spiritual wisdom.

Fravashi: spark of the divine (from Ahura Mazda).

Diagram of the Soul

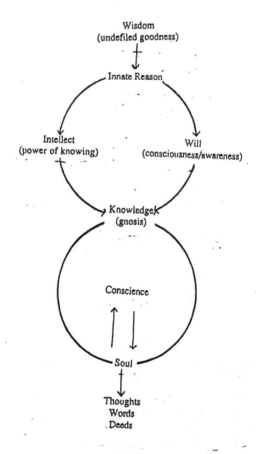

Understanding the intricacies of the complex understanding of what makes up the individual human being according to ancient Iranian teachings can take a great deal of inner spiritual work. It is offered here for informational purposes only. It is not necessary to understand these ideas right now. The Good Religion can be practiced on many levels. Knowledge and experience in the more subtle realms of the human body-mind complex can lead to more effective prayer and ritual effectiveness. (It should be noted in passing that this system is very similar to all other Indo-European systems, including that of the ancient Celts and Germans.)

One of the questions humankind most often asks of its religions and spiritual traditions is: What happens after death? Most religions have an answer for this question, and the Good Religion is no exception. The major answers are found by logically following certain ideas: God created humankind to help in the war on the onslaught of evil in the world. Human souls incarnated from a heavenly or "spiritual" state (*menog*) and will return there upon death. The souls were created by God as pure entities, and so were the bodies which humans first inhabited. Both are equally good creations of the Wise Lord. Logically, first of all, each human will find eternal salvation, because he or she is a volunteer to fight for Ahura Mazda in the war on evil. Any shortcomings of individuals will be purified after death. All deeds are recorded in the human soul and the *daena* of that soul will be its own judge. There is no need here and now to discuss the repercussions of that judgment. We know that we are the creations of the Wise Lord, that he is Good and only created things which are essentially good. In the end all good things will resolve to their original state of goodness, power and integrity. Some religions see man as *essentially* a "damned sinner," whereas the Good Religion sees man as an essentially good being capable of being temporarily led astray by bad thoughts, words and deeds.

Chapter 8
Ethics and Philosophy

It is clear that the ethical system of the Good Religion can be summed up in the three words: *Humata-Hukhta-Khvarsta*— Good Thoughts, Good Words, Good Deeds. This is simply profound. But is not as simple as it might appear. In many ways this Zarathustran ethical system was a sophisticated analysis of the ancient Indo-European code of honor. The three-word formula has to be analyzed in order to be fully understood, but the simplicity of this three-word formula has allowed it to stand the test of time and to be transmitted throughout the world in different guises.

As we have seen, the early Greeks took much of the basic ideology they expressed in what came to be called "philosophy" from the Persians, and specifically from the doctrines of Zarathustra. They secularized them insofar as they developed a system of thought more or less independent of the world of their native gods and goddesses whereas Zarathustra worked from within such a system and reformed it into a holistic religio-philosophical structure.

The concept of the Good as a philosophical principle is central to the ideology of Zarathustra, and it identified with the essence of the Wise Lord. The Greek philosopher Plato made it his highest principle, called in Greek the *Agathon*. The Agathon is also identical with the Light, or Being, in different systems. All of these systems agree with, and are derived from, Zarathustran teachings. The Good is all things which are or promote absolute wisdom, knowledge, truth, honesty, happiness joy, pleasure, constructiveness, health, benefit, prosperity, order, kindness and life. Fundamental to the workings of the Good is the principle of the Golden Mean or moderation. Most things in life have their right place, but anything in excess or deficiency is bad.

Now that we have an idea of what the Good is, what is Evil? The principle of Evil is understood as the diametrical opposite of each of these things. These are things we know that exist: ignorance, falsehood, misery, despair, pain, destruction, illness, harmfulness, poverty, chaos, greed and death. It is Man's function in the world to fight these negative impulses, in his own life and in the world in general.

So often when we hear the word "evil," we place it in the context of Christian church-ideas about such things: "evil" is felt to tinge things Man enjoys— sex, prosperity, intoxication, gambling, etc. The Church taught, many things were sins which are indeed bad, such as lying, cheating, murdering, etc., but even now when one thinks of the Christian idea of "sin," it brings to mind things people enjoy, but "shouldn't." The Mazdan idea of sin is steadfast and certain, but not much like the Christian one. The Churchman taught people to abstain from thoughts, words and acts which were categorically said to be sinful.

But the Mazdan way holds that sin is the commission of an evil thought, word, or action and evil is thought of as something which is either *excessive* or *deficient*. The Mean is the Good, and it is just the right amount of something, not too much and not too little. It is the excess or deficiency which manifests the daevic aspect. Almost everything can be good in the right amount, at the right time and in the right place. To judge these things requires insight, reason and wisdom. It seems easier to just say do *this*, and don't do *that*. But as history has shown, such a "philosophy" can lead to evil in itself— spiritual blindness, stupidity and insanity.

The bedrock of Mazdan ethics is summed up in the formula *humata-hukhta-khvarsta*: Good Thoughts, Good Words, Good Deeds. Each of these concepts needs to be examined in some detail before their entire meaning can be fully appreciated.

Upon first hearing of the Good Religion's emphasis of the very word "good," many modern people probably think at first that the religion is obsessed with being "goody-two-shoes." This notion is dispelled as soon as one digs a bit deeper into the real meaning of the concept. The Good in question is not about being "nice," or following rules out of a love for rules, rather the Good is a matter of high quality and integrity which gives pure power to the universe and the individual. When we say: "That is a good horse," we do not mean that it is well-behaved or gentle, we mean more that it is swift, powerful, courageous and well-trained to do its tasks. The Good in question is a matter of the proper fulfilling of functions. Aristotle would say that an eye is "in its Good when it sees," or "a foot is in its Good when it walks," because that it was these organs were made to do. They do these actions better than other organs. Man himself is "in his Good" when he *thinks*. When we say "Good Thoughts," for example, we do not necessarily mean "nicy-nice" thoughts, but rather high-quality and integral thoughts. As a matter of fact such thoughts lead a person to be more honest, truthful and loving toward others, but these are not the primary aim of the Good Thoughts, just inevitable by-products of them.

Humata
Good Thoughts

Again it has to be emphasized that the word "good" has different connotations in Mazdan (and general Indo-European) terminology than it does in conventional Christian jargon. Something which is good is powerful and effective, true to its nature and authentic, as well as being infused with wisdom and consciousness. A Good Thought is a complex thing. It will be generally characterized by being concentrated, vivid, inherited, serene, meaningful, logical and inspired. If these qualities are present in the thought, and are pursued for their own sake, the thought will also be characterized as being ethical and promoting of ethical words and deeds. One will become not only more effective and powerful in all that one does, one will also become more charitable, kind and loving in one's thoughts toward one's fellow man, and toward all of the other Creations of the Wise Lord.

In order to pursue the acquisition of Good Thoughts one should undergo training in concentration, visualization, memorization, meditation, contemplation and logic/reasoning. Most essentially also, however, one should pursue avenues of opening one's self to the flow of inspiration that comes from the *yazatas* and Ahura Mazda as well as from his Creations. This element of inspiration is most readily acquired through formal prayer-rituals performed in the presence of Atar on a daily basis. This is the true root of Magic.

The Seven Virtues, or ethical concepts in the Mazdan Way, which lead from thoughts to deeds, are:

1. Good-mind
2. Wisdom
3. Truthfulness and Righteous Deeds
4. Self-Reliance and Autonomy
5. Peace and Serenity
6. Wholeness and Excellence
7. Perseverance and Steadfastness

The spiritual quest of the individual in the Good Religion is to uncover the essence of wisdom (Phl. *khrad*) by training the mind to seek it. K. P. Mistree writes: "God is Wisdom whose inherent nature is to further the 'gnosis' of this world. Wisdom needs no Creator, as Wisdom *is*, for it affirms itself to itself." (p. 43) Khrad can also be translated as "innate reason." This is a rational faculty of the soul which is the gateway to inner wisdom. This is not gained by blind faith in authority, but rather through the exercise of the mind and soul in relation to life and the world.

As time goes on and the faculties of mind and soul are exercised and honed through rigorous discipline, Insight (Av. *daena*) begins to be gained. This is because true religion is seen as the product of Insight developed from within the soul, rather than rules and regulations imposed from without.

Good Thoughts are the true and authentic basis of Good Words.

Hukhta
Good Words

Good Words are not merely the disciplined use of language so as not to offend others, although this may be a minor byproduct that naturally flows from the virtue in question. Good Words are rather the direct product of Good Thoughts as described above. Words are crystalized, articulated and conscious manifestations of thoughts. Many people may have Good Thoughts but have not developed the faculty to translate them into articulated words. Thus the thoughts are trapped and cannot have their proper effect in the world or among the person's fellow humans. This restriction must be broken so that the Good Words can flow both inwardly and outwardly.

To have and express Good Words, one must practice discipline in spoken articulation of language and hone one's skills in pronunciation and self-expression through language. Words are vehicles for *communication* of ideas or thoughts. Thoughts can just exist in one brain, but words are necessary to convey information from one mind to another. This process is essential in the fight against destructive forces by means of teaching and learning.

Beyond this, however, are the Good Words which form the *mathras* more commonly referred to as "prayers." Also, the words contained in the sacred scriptures in Avestan, Pahlavi and Modern Persian texts convey a body of Good Words which should be studied and understood.

These *mathras*, or words of power, are the bridge between thoughts and actions. They are the mode by which thoughts are spread from one person to another. These are essential weapons in the struggle for the constant improvement of ourselves, society and the world around us.

Good Words are the prototypes of Good Deeds.

Khvarshta
Good Deeds

Khvarshta stems from *Humata* and *Hukhta*. Good Actions are the follow-through of the groundwork laid by Good Thoughts and Good Words. Good Actions are necessary to the fight against the forces of destruction in our world. Merely having good and serene thoughts or being "enlightened" in a passive way is not enough. The Mazdan Way is a robust and virile way. It is a plan of action, not merely meditation or contemplation. The inner work is a prelude to outer action. All are necessary to the endeavor, but without Good Deeds the thoughts and words are impotent. Good Deeds are things one does in the outer objective world which are motivated by Good Thoughts and formulated by Good Words. A Good Action is one that is measurable, visible, or audible, and which makes a positive difference in the world around the doer of that action.

Good Words can exist purely articulated in someone's mind, they can be written in private papers, put when the words are spoken to another person, or shared among other people in written or recorded form they become acts, and are thus categorized as Good Deeds as well as Good Words.

One system of Good Deeds is the series of Seven Acts of Piety which every follower of the Good Religion should strive to actualize on a daily basis. These are especially to be practiced during the obligatory times of celebration known as Gahambars. These Acts of Piety are:

1. Generosity of spirit (including speaking well of others)
2. Material generosity and sharing
3. Honesty
4. Community participation and inclusion (including supporting Gahambars)
5. Selfless help toward those in need (without desire for recognition or reward)
6. Faithfulness and Piety
7. Remembrance of the souls of the righteous ones and ancestors

Good actions are those which promote absolute wisdom, knowledge, truth, honesty, happiness, joy, pleasure, constructiveness, health, benefit, prosperity, order, kindness and life. This is especially true when these are for the benefit of others or the world at large. Each of these actions is a martial act against the daevic forces which withers a part of their effectiveness. When all people are, by their own inner consciences, directed toward these acts, the time of Making Wonderful will be at hand.

Charity

(Ahlavdad)

Here I have given the Pahlavi word for "charity" to make this virtue more clear. Although we live in a society being increasingly "charitable" in a coerced sort of way through our governmental institutions, we still have a cultural aversion to the word "charity." The Pahlavi word clarifies that this virtue is merely *doing the right thing.* In Pahlavi *dad* means "law" or "code of conduct," while *ahlav* means "righteous." We are charitable not to make ourselves "feel better," or to "alleviate our guilt," but simply because it is righteous law to practice it. Essential to the message of Zarathustra is the care for the oppressed and impoverished. They may need education, a helping friend, a hot meal, a friendly gesture, but whatever it is, the Mazdan feels obligated to try to provide it. This may be one of the driving forces behind the prosperity of the modern-day Parsees in India. If you are highly desirous of being able to afford to give to the less fortunate, then you are bound to become rich yourself. Not that wealth was the goal, but it can be the end result with the help of the Bounteous Immortals. Meet your own responsibilities to yourself, to your family and then to your community. You want to be able to give back to the community, but you cannot do so wisely before you have taken care of things at home (within the bounds of the Golden Mean, of course).

The Environment

Of the Seven Creations, fully six of them make up the *environment* of humanity: the water, earth, plants, animals and even the sky (atmosphere) and fire are parts of the natural surroundings of humanity on this planet. Mazdans therefore are natural environmentalists. We want to protect and defend the environment in *partnership* with Man, not the detriment of Man with regard to the environment. Mazdans see Mankind and our place in the Seven Creations as an essential part of the whole. The Bogomil or Gnostic wing of the environmentalist movement, which sees humanity as the problem, runs contrary to the Mazdan Way. The environment must be engineered by human genius for the betterment of all Seven Creations. That is the holistic goal. The simple elimination of human existence is contrary to Mazdan teachings.

The Green movement can only succeed once a spiritual and intellectual framework has been established which grows from the same roots as does the environmental movement itself. Mainstream Judeo-Christian tradition is well-known to be at the base of many of the negative practices contrary to the Green philosophy— exploitation of the environment for the excessive and exclusive benefit of human kind. Some have toyed with paganism, falsely believing that pagans were simple "nature worshippers." But such a path is arbitrary and without deep conviction. It can with honesty be said that the Good Religion is an entirely Green form of spirituality.

An important Zoroastrian writer, Mistree, once wrote that after the Zoroastrian has prepared himself ethically and through other spiritual practices he:

"... begins to gain an insight into the workings of the physical world. Through this insight an awareness of, and a responsibility towards, the Wise Lord's creations begin to emerge, resulting in a Zoroastrian championing the cause of ecology against those responsible for the pollution and defilement of all that is natural and good in the world. God's world must be kept pure and because of the importance of the general well-being of man in his world, a Zoroastrian is encouraged to live life to its fullest, in order that he may learn to preserve and enjoy the goodness of the seven creations. Monasticism, fasting, celibacy and mortification of the body, are an anathema to a Zoroastrian as it is believed that such practices weaken man and thereby lessen his power to fight evil. Similarly pessimism and despair are sins are in fact are seen as yielding to evil. The task of man is to learn to combat evil with courage, moral fortitude and affirmation."

(Zoroastrianism, p. 18)

It should be apparent that this ancient faith forms the perfect and natural theoretical model for a true Green spirituality.

Human Rights

Individuals and naturally unified groups of peoples (families, clans, tribes and nations) have the natural right to self-determination. Each has the right ot make his, her, or its own choices. The idea of choice is fundamental to the Mazdan Way. But the fact that the choice is relative, does not mean that the Truth is relative. The Truth cannot be arrived at by force. Foȑ this reason the Mazdan Way promotes the rights of individuals and groups to make their own free choices.

Mazdan ideas of human rights stem from the general principle, revolutionary in the ancient world, that the Wise Lord — as the focused form of consciousness — is the *one* and *only* absolute God, and as such is the God of all mankind, not just of one particular tribe or people. Historical events caused the Zoroastrian message to be sequestered in an ethnic model, but this was not the original idea. If all humanity is here to fight for the Good (even if they have forgotten it) then they should all have the same rights and respect. Most of mankind is, however, beset with ignorance (the effects of the infection of Ahriman). How can they be brought to the Light? They cannot be taught to love by punishing them with hate and destruction. The Truth abhors coercion. We must arrive at the Truth through Insight, Reason and Wisdom. Giving in to coercion is a temptation that the Persians did not resist during periods of the Sasanian Empire, which was a dire mistake.

The most perfect historical exponent of Zarathustrian principles was Cyrus (Kurush) the Great. He is now most famous in the West for his cuneiform seal (a copy which is displayed at the United Nations Headquarters in New York) which is a declaration of his tolerance policy toward the newly conquered Babylonians in 539 BCE. The last Shah of Iran touted the seal as the oldest human rights document in history. His respect for the peoples of his empire stemmed from his Mazdan faith. Contrary to the image projected in anti-Persian Greek propaganda, the Persian Emperors were generally kind and benevolent toward their peoples. Slavery was not the manpower used to build the great cities, but rather fair wages were paid to skilled workers in exchange for their services. His idea in all things was that free people, exercising their free choice was a more ideal state of affairs than any other. As a ruler he would practice the reverse of the principle of Machiavelli who said a ruler should be feared and not loved, with Cyrus it was better to be loved than feared. People cooperated with him and his plans largely because they wanted to, not because he forced them.

Because one of the most fundamental tenets of the ancient Zarathustrian mission was the defense of the oppressed and powerless (no matter to which of the Seven Creations they belong) present-day Mazdans often find themselves involved in efforts to help these. We do these things because they are right, but also because they are vigorous acts of combat against the daevic impulse toward ignorance, violence and cruelty. The Mazdan always feeds the poor, the Mazdan always stands up to the bully, the Mazdan always teaches the Truth.

Ahriman today has many tools and weapons by which he limits human rights and choice. The main one is the crippling of the very part of the human soul that is capable of making real choices— the daevic attack on humanity on a physical, emotional, economic, political and spiritual level is highly sophisticated. Mankind is led to believe choices are being made, when in fact only stimulated responses are being experienced. Human rights are good and necessary, but they begin within the soul of each individual who must freely develop his spirit into one capable of making real choices before human rights can really be enjoyed.

Women's Rights

Zarathustra has been credited as the first champion of women's rights because he established the full and equal initiation of girls into the faith, whereas all other tribal traditions had strictly divided the initiation of boys and girls. Boys were the only ones really initiated into the tribal tradition in a complete way. Zarathustra was the first to break this pattern, and as such he was the first to open the door to the possibility of equality.

In traditional eastern Zoroastrianism the priesthood is an all-male, hereditary office. Only sons of priests can become priests. This is an ancient principle, but one which is untenable and impractical in the West.

In the Occidental Temple of the Wise Lord it has been mandated that the priesthood is open to all who will undergo the educational and spiritual requirements to assume that office. This includes women.

In this we feel that we are extending in a logical way the principle of equality established by Zarathustra in the beginning.

Animal Rights

Although Zarathustra began his mission in part as a protest against the excessive and/or wrongly performed animal sacrifices being made by the warrior-class in his time and area, in general the Indo-European mindset is one which already intrinsically recognized the value of what he was saying. Indo-Europeans sacrificed animals, but they ate the meat of the sacrificed animals. It can be said that the only difference between now and then was that the slaughtering process was considered a sacred act in ancient times, and now it is just a commercial operation. Part of the sacred aspect included the idea that the animals were raised humanely and slaughtered in ways in which they were to suffer no fear or pain— this was because the animals were seen as physical reflections of divine forces. To cause the animal pain or fear was to cause discomfort to the god or goddess who had manifested the animal for mankind. That would be no way to win their favors! The Greeks said the animal had to consent to be sacrificed. In the Germanic world the idea of "over-sacrifice" is addressed in the "Hávamál" where the god who corresponds to the position of the Wise Lord in that pantheon says:

"Better unasked than over-offered

... better unsent than over-sacrificed." (Hávamál 145.)

In the Gathas Zarathustra pleads for the "Soul of the Ox." This is poignant as it was the "Soul of the Ox" which had pleaded with the Wise Lord to send Zarathustra to Mankind to show us the way to victory over Ahriman. The "Soul of the Ox" is the spiritual construct embracing the beings of all of the animal world, in their individual and collective manifestations.

Although the animal world is represented by the "Soul of the Ox" the highest place in the animal kingdom is reserved for the dog. It is said that evil cannot abide the gaze of a dog. In the funeral ceremony the dead body, shown to a special dog who looks at the body to drive away evil influences. This view of the dog is called the *sagdid*. Zoroastrians like to have dogs as companions as well as working partners. Dogs are given a portion of the meal eaten by humans. The lore of the "Z-dog" will be addressed in more detail in a later study. The main reason the dog is recognized for special consideration is that it is only the dog in the animal world who will obey his master and actually *enjoy* doing so. This is the attitude of a good human toward engaging in battle in the world on the behalf of the Wise Lord.

It is part of the core mission of the OTWL to promote animal rights and the humane treatment of animals across the planet. We encourage local efforts in this regard everywhere and usually have as a part of our local operations some sort of active and practical charitable programs for the care of abused or abandoned creatures.

Health and Happiness

The Good Religion teaches us that one of the goals of human life is to attain the most perfect state of happiness possible. The ancient term for "happiness" is *ushta*. One of the essential components of this state is health and well-being. Mazdan health consists of three levels: spirit (*mainyu*), mind (*manah*) and body (*tanu*). Health is approached both from the spiritual and the material (*gaetha*) direction.

Many religions have various ideas on practices which involve the maintenance of human health. Some have at various times suggested that there is something "spiritual" about starving or mortifying the body. Others have strict dietary laws of food which are forbidden to eat. The Good Religion has definite teachings on all of this, but it might be unexpected.

Because Zarathustra taught the inherent goodness of the material or physical creation, because he wanted humankind to enjoy life, and because he wanted his incarnated warriors to be vital and strong in their struggle for the Good, he rejected the idea that you should starve or mortify your body for any "spiritual" purpose. The human body should be strengthened and should enjoy pleasure. Our pleasures are the pleasures of the Wise Lord. Of course, this is not to say that the Prophet taught hedonism. Far from it! He promoted a difficult path, that of *moderation*. Nothing is forbidden, but nothing is to be indulged in to any excess. By the same token, everything is to be enjoyed, everything without deficiency. This can be a more difficult path than following the *kosher* or *halal* laws of Judaism or Islam. But it avoids the promotions of either gluttony or asceticism found in Christianity.

Some modern Zoroastrians are vegetarians, but this is not commanded by their religion. Their vegetarianism is born of health concerns to some degree, but is motivated more by a desire not to cause or promote cruelty to innocent life. Some rank the acceptability of eating the meat of certain animals in a very specific way. We know that there are certain populations around the world that will swallow just about anything. In general Indo-Europeans have among themselves very similar ideas about what is acceptable and not. The Zoroastrian code is thought out according to certain philosophical principles. If animals are highly conscious creatures, for example, dogs or swine, or play an important part in the mythology of the faith, for example roosters or cattle, then their meat is less desirable. The most favored meats are fish and chicken. For and interesting discussion of these matters see orthodoxzoroastrianism.wordpress.com. The dietary "laws" are these: make yourself strong and vital, indulge in nothing to excess and deprive yourself of nothing so that you will suffer from a deficiency. Be kind to animals. Avoid eating the meat of intelligent and noble animals (for example dogs and horses). Eat meat that has been prepared humanely. Any animal which is slaughtered should suffer no fear or pain in the process. (This is an ancient Indo-European concept that pre-dates even Zoroastrianism, although the ignoring of this precept may have been one of the traits that Zarathustra protested against in his lifetime.)

The Good Religion has some definite practices and ideas on the promotion of health and the healing of maladies. We emphasize a holistic lifestyle in which all parts of the individual are properly cared for and maintained. The two major approaches are the *haoma*-discipline (herbalism) combined with *mathra*-practices. The latter are prayers taken from holy scripture which have the effect of maintaining and restoring health and wellbeing. Also key to this overall approach is the constant practice of the virtue of *moderation*.

It is considered essential to maintain good bodily health and strength, because a healthy body is necessary support the spirit which is able to carry out the fight that each individual has ideally been incarnated to carry out.

Gardens

We have already seen how the global and universal environment, composed of the Seven Creations, is so important to practitioners of the Good Religion. A healthy environment makes it possible for all of humanity to grow and prosper. On a smaller scale Mazdans are known to cultivate spaces which enhance tranquility, pleasure and comfort. These are the famous Zoroastrian or Persian Gardens. In Persian such a garden is known as a *bagh*. They are modeled on our knowledge of the structure of heaven. The word "Paradise" comes from the Old Persian *paridaiza*, "a walled garden or park." One of the most typical designs for these gardens is one which is divided by four water courses. It is this image which is evoked in the description of the Garden of Eden in Genesis. Persian Gardens are designed to be cool in the hot arid environment of the Iranian Plateau. There are several possible design principles in the design and building of a Persian Garden space. They can be as big as several acres or as small as the patio behind your apartment. They create spaces for personal prayer and meditation, interpersonal interaction and aesthetic appreciation. Being within these spaces promotes health and wellbeing on all levels. As a way to promote health and happiness on all levels, regular retreats to these spaces are recommended.

One of the oldest known formal Persian Gardens is found at the ruins of Cyrus the Great's capital city Pasargad. Its design shows the archetype of the best form of a garden of this type. Gardening was so important to the Zoroastrian emperors of Persia that they wanted to be remembered first as gardeners, then as emperors. It should be a goal of followers of the Good Religion to create their own personal garden spaces and to propagate the construction of such gardens everywhere.

Cultivation of Plants

From the Legend of the Grain we learn that it is thought that Zarathustra himself cultivated a garden or orchard. The story also implies that this garden was the site of his school of philosophy where the future *athravans* were being trained. Zarathustra saw the cultivation of useful plants as an exercise in the practice of the Truth. It is a peaceful, non-injurious, method of producing food. When arranged in a garden, plants help create an environment which is healthy and provides an atmosphere of pleasure and happiness for those who tarry within the garden walls.

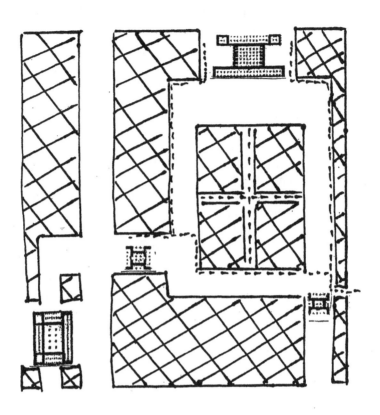

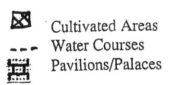

Cultivated Areas
Water Courses
Pavilions/Palaces

Design of the Garden at Pasargad

From a religious perspective it is seen that the follower of the Good Religion should make an effort to cultivate useful and beautiful plants. This could be as simple as a box of tomatoes or a flower bed in front of your house. But aspire to do more if at all possible. Ideally you will raise enough food to feed not only yourself, but also be able to give some of the food away to friends or to the poor.

Child Rearing

As with all things, the Good Religion does not command people to have children. Such a command would violate the principle of the Mean. It is simply said that it is *better* to have children than not to have them. Of course, it is understood that we are talking about only bringing children into loving homes with the resources to raise them well.

It is the obligation of a parent to show by example what it is to be a follower of the Good Religion. Children should not be coerced, either overtly or covertly, to become members of the faith. Anyone motivated by fear or pain to do something, or to behave in a certain way, is not being allowed the freedom of conscience necessary to make the *choice* to do the Good. The Occidental Temple does not accept full members under the age of eighteen, although children are, of course, welcome and included in all activities. The choice to become a member must be made freely with a mind which has developed a high level of conscience.

RITUAL AND PRAYER

How to Become a Follower of the Good Religion

It is not necessary to abandon whatever faith or creed you are presently following, if any, to begin the journey into the Good Religion. But you must make some commitment to the faith, otherwise you can expect little to no benefit from your efforts. Our message is that you must do the Good for the sake of the Good without expectation of reward. However, your conscious mind, if it is ready to believe what we say here, needs to acknowledge the Truth. If you do not, you are feeding the Lie. If what we say is true, it is certainly worthy of your commitment to its message. These truths have been more or less manifested in various religions of the past, but nowhere are they to be found in their purity and strength more than in the Good Religion itself. To make the first commitment to the faith, and begin to undertake thoughts, words and actions in harmony with its principles, you should recite the following formula in the presence of at least one human witness:

> In the name of the Wise Lord,
> who is benevolent and kind:
> Praise be to the message of Zarathustra,
> sent by God to this world.
> I seek to remember who I am.
> I stand ready to fight for Good.
> I believe, know and understand that truth,
> first revealed by Zarathustra.
> Let the Good Religion guide me.
> *Humata-Hukhta-Hvarshta*
> [hoomata-hookhta-wharshta]
> Good Thoughts–Good Words–Good Deeds.

After one has made this formulaic statement before a witness, one can consider one's self a follower of the Good Religion. To advance in one's spirituality it will be desirable to become an initiate of the Temple and by formally affiliating with it and undergoing initiation. Remember, however, that this does not make you a "Zoroastrian." We are not Zoroastrians, *per se*, but rather Mazdans. This recitation makes you a Mazdan and follower of the teachings of Zarathustra. It does not demand that you reject any other faith or religious tradition, but over time and through learning and experience most will gain insight and come to understand the best and highest truth which the Mazdan Way represents. Even then tribal or culturally conventional forms of religion may still form a part of a person's social, political and family life.

Chapter 9
Ritual and Household Ceremony

Basic Theory and Practice

Because eastern Zoroastrianism had its origin with a professional ritual priest, which Zarathustra was, and because it has been guided by professional a priesthood steeped in ritual training for almost four thousand years, eastern orthodox Zoroastrianism is a highly ritualized religion. In the West, even in Indo-European pagan times, rituals were never as elaborate as they became in the east, whether in Iran or India. For this and other reasons, rituals under the auspices of the Occidental Temple of the Wise Lord are not as elaborate or lengthy as those found in the east.

Ritual is necessary and essential to the practice of the Good Religion. K. P. Mistree writes:

> Rituals are a set of practices which when enacted in a given prescribed order, become the medium through which a person is able to relate to an unseen spiritual world. It is through a ritual that an individual existentially experiences a link between the physical and spiritual worlds. A ritual also enables one to maintain a continuity of religious experience with the past.

(Zoroastrianism, p. 60)

Through ritual practice and recitation of the *mathras*, the individual forges a link with the spiritual world and thus transforms the world into a more spiritual state in a real and direct way. The one who performs the ritual or recites the *mathra* aims to generate ritual power (*amal*). To do so the ritual actions must be performed with full concentration, right intention combined with a virtuous mind.

In performing rituals and reciting *mathras*, the celebrant brings joy to the fravashis of the departed and to the gods and goddesses, and most especially to the Amesha Spentas and the Wise Lord himself.

Rituals are of two major types: those which are practiced alone or by an individual independent of a group, and those which are necessarily done in a group or which require at least two people to perform.

Individual Ritual

An individual ritual is one which is practiced alone. In these instances there is no need for any other person to complete all necessary ritual obligations. These form the body of the major daily rituals a

Mazdan might perform. These are the daily prayers before the Fire (Atash). Such rituals can be done in groups or by several people simultaneously, but this is not their primary use or intention. Each individual or family should have their own household shrine, shelf or ritual table at which they perform their daily rituals or prayers.

The typical bodily posture for prayer is standing upright with your elbows touching your sides and your forearms angled away with upturned palms. The greatest effect is obtained when reciting *mathras* from memory while gazing into the heart of Atar.

Group Ritual

Group rituals are those in which more than one participant is virtually *necessary*. This necessity stems from two sources: the need for another participant to complete the ritual procedures (for example the *Gahambar* ritual) or those which are essentially communal in nature. Because of the social character of the Good Religion, it is not ideally practiced by isolated individuals. The most profound ancient symbol of Mazdaism, the eternal flames of the Fire Temples in Iran and India which have been kept burning continuously in some instances for as long as a thousand years, are social or *cultural* symbols. Such continuity requires a team of individuals to tend the fire several times a day, every day, throughout the year, and from year to year. The existence of such fires is a testimony to the strength of the tradition and a symbol of cultural continuity.

The chief type of rites which need to be performed in a group are the *Gahambars*. This is mainly because the performance of the rite itself involves a minimum of two persons. Additionally the full meaning of the entire ritual of the *Gahambars* can only be appreciated in a social setting. This includes group participation in the preparation for the rite as well as the distribution of food to people outside the community who might have need of it.

As this book is mainly intended for the lay-member of the Temple of the Wise Lord, as well as those trying the forms and practices as a personal and private exploration, all rituals presented in any detail will be those of a household variety. Rituals of the kind held in formal Temple-services conducted by a priest of the Temple are not presented here.

All rites generally involve three main parts: 1) the preparation for the ritual (which usually takes a day or so before the actual rite), 2) the rite itself, and 3) the party and distribution of food which follows.

The format for the festival ritual used for the six Gahambars and the New Year celebration has seven parts. First the objects and ritual space are prepared and arranged in their proper order. The formal ritual begins with the purification of the participants. The concept of "purity" is often misunderstood. Mistree writes:

Purity is the inherent quality that reflects the goodness of God in the physical, psychological and spiritual worlds. In Zoroastrianism, purity is closely linked to the concept of *asha*— order, truth and righteousness. It is purity of thought, word and deed that makes a man follow the path of *asha*. Purity, therefore, is the experiential dimension of truth.

(Zoroastrianism, p. 62)

Purity is both the elimination of pollution (which weakens the system it pollutes) and the maximization of strength and vitality characterized by strong order. For the ancients purity was a method of attaining and maintaining power. In church-based Christianity, perhaps, purity is sought so that the Christian God may look with favor upon the individual, whereas in the Mazdan Way purity a method provided by the Wise Lord to strengthen us and lead us toward Truth.

The most simple format for a group ritual is that used for the *Gahambars* in the OTWL. The steps are as follow:

0. Preparation of Ritual Objects and Space
1. Purification and Preparation of Active Celebrants
2. Lighting of Fire
3. Opening Prayers
4. Recitations of Purpose
   a) For the specific purpose of the festival
   b) For remembrance of the ancestors and heroes
5. Consecration of Consumables and Exchange of Flowers
6. Solemn and Silent Consumption of Sacralized Food and Drink
7. Closing Prayers

The steps of this ritual will be explained in detail in chapter 12. It is the fifth and sixth steps of the ritual which absolutely requires a second person to complete the purpose of the ritual. In that section there is an exchange between two celebrants of symbolic objects, most usually flowers. The two also engage in ceremonial handshakes or other acts of symbolic connection. The oldest known representations of the now-common Western social custom of shaking hands are found in depictions of Mithra shaking hands with his human compatriots.

Chapter 10
Tools and Setting

As we learned earlier, in the most ancient times the original Zoroastrians worshipped in the open air, usually on high grounds such as hilltops or mountaintops, or even in caves and grottos, etc. They also did so at sea shores and other places of natural beauty. No images were ever made of Ahura Mazda. Again these descriptions sound very similar to ones of the early Germanic peoples. By the time the religion became established among Persian kings and emperors, however, more elaborate temples and complexes were being built in which to perform the rituals. But forever and always the simple forms of worship were still practiced and have had high prestige.

Regardless of the overall setting, however, certain tools and implements are necessary to the proper performance of a typical Mazdan ritual.

The space in which the ritual takes place must be as free as possible of any non-sacred objects or furniture. Traditionally lines are demarcated on the floor in the following pattern shown in the diagram below:

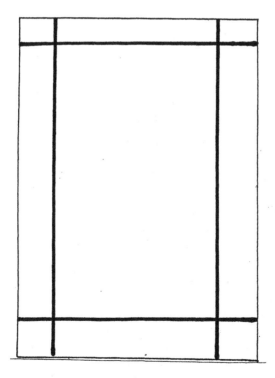

The lines are formulated to divert any negative, destructive or detrimental influences from entering the space within the lines.

Here follows a list of ritual objects or tools useful for most basic rites in the Mazdan tradition:

Fire Vase
(afrinagan)

The most famous ceremonial object of Mazdan ritual is the fire vase or urn. It can be of various sizes and designs. Most usually the vase is made of a silver-colored metal. A metal dish or plate of the right size is placed on its top and the ceremonial fire is built on top of this. Ashes from the fire have a special magical property, and cannot be disposed of in a disrespectful manner. The fire used to light the fuel on the *afrinagan* comes from the oil lamp.

Oil Lamp
(divo)

The oil lamp is a container filled with lamp oil and fitted with a floating wick. A substitute for this can be a small candle or tea-light. It should be able to burn throughout the ritual and be the representative of the eternal flame. No fire should be actively extinguished. Fire should always be allowed to burn itself out on its own.

Fuel and Incense
(aesma-bui)

The ritual Fire (Atar) is fed with both wooden fuel and incense during rituals. The usual fuel is made up of well-dried sticks of wood. This can be juniper or mountain cedar or especially in the Indian tradition it is usually sandalwood. It is important that this wood be very dry. Burning moist wood is thought to be a moral detriment. The incense used is most usually frankincense (*loban*) and/or myrrh (*bod*).

Metal Ladle
(chamach)

The ladle is a long handled tool with a somewhat flat scoop for placing incense on the fire. This process is done at certain prescribed times in some rituals, but can be done at any point in order to keep the sacralizing effect of the incense present in the atmosphere of the ritual.

Metal Tongs
(chipyo)

Metal tongs are used to place supplemental wood on the fire. The fire is normally built with extremely dry wood (usually juniper or sandalwood). The fire may need to be fed with more wood to keep it burning healthily throughout the ritual. If and when this is the case, it is to be fed with wood of this kind using the metal tongs.

Head-Cover
(*topi*)
The typical head-covering for the Zoroastrian is a bill-less cap which covers the whole top of the head, not a "skullcap" as used by the Jews. Many designs are possible. the only prerequisite is that the material be white.

White Table Cover
(*sofreh*)
The altar-table is to be covered by a white cloth. This cloth should only be used for this purpose and must be clean each time it is used.

Altar Table
(*khwan*)
The altar-table itself should be a four-legged table. It can be of any height and surface dimensions as desired or needed. Some are quite small, while others can be very large. It depends on the number of people involved and the level of elaboration desired.

Bowls, Dishes and Trays
Various offerings or displays of things such as bread, water, fruits, nuts, milk, honey, etc. are to be contained in ceremonial dishes, bowls and trays. These are most usually made out of metal (brass, "German Silver" or stainless steel) or they are earthenware. It is important for symbolic reasons to keep these objects pure and apart from daily use in any other context. The circular bowl containing pure water is called the *kundi*.

Picture of the Prophet Zarathustra
There is a variety of idealized and obviously symbolic "portraits" of the Prophet Zarathustra. He is seen as the ideal man, the representative of what all humans can and will be in the end. His image, therefore, is representative not only of his message to mankind, but also of the future state toward which we aspire.

Chapter 11
Daily Rituals and Prayer

Basic Personal Frame Rituals and Prayers

The practice of a religion is both personal or private and communal or group oriented. As mentioned previously there are practices for individuals and groups. The individual practices tend to be ones that are done every day, while group activities are generally reserved for seasonal or calendrical festivals or celebrations.

At its most basic level Mazdan ritual consists of the recitation of certain *mathras* or prayers while gazing upon an open flame. Depending on the level of dedication or spiritual devotion of the individual these rituals may be more or less elaborate. Many Mazdans, like other Zarathustrians, emphasize ethical action in their spiritual lives, while others concentrate more on inner work. Here, as in all things, moderation and balance is the optimum, we should think.

In orthodox eastern Zoroastrianism there exist complex and lengthy prayers and rituals for daily practice. As this text is an introduction to basic history, theory and practice we will keep the rituals and *mathras* to a minimum. The most important thing is to learn to focus and refocus on the basic ideas and practices of the Good Religion. Future works will deepen the level of practice.

To begin any formal individual ritual activity the hands and face should be washed with clean water, and the mouth rinsed with the same. Place a covering on your head, preferably a white prayer cap, or *topi*. It is *best* to be dressed in an all-white set of garments when praying before Atar. This is because the color white naturally reflects and deflects all detrimental influences from the minions of Ahriman. After these purifications are complete, stand before your ritual table and light your ceremonial flame while reciting: *Yazdān ni Yād* ("In honor and to the glory of the Creator").

Now move on to whatever ritual or prayer you have to perform.

The Nature of Prayer

When we hear the word "prayer" it probably calls forth notions of Western church prayer, which can often be a kind of groveling or wheedling before a judgmental father figure. This is in no way the case in Mazdan "prayer." The Avestan words for "prayer" are *spenta mathra*, literally "holy words," and *yasna*, which means "worship," that is, "paying respects to, or honoring something." The *Avesta* consists almost entirely of such holy words. They are not literary works nearly as much as they are magical mantras (*mathras*). This is why they continue to be recited in the Avestan language and often cannot be fully or accurately translated. Their real meaning is more in the power of their effects, rather than the literal definitions of the words and sentences. The *mathras* are vehicles of communication between the world of man and that of the Wise Lord and the *yazatas*.

A *mathra* links the mind of man to that of the Wise Lord and to the very fabric of the universe shaped by God. This linkage is one to which the human mind and the divine mind are predisposed, simply because the divine mind is the common origin of all individual human minds and souls. The major *mathras*, as described below, are analyzed in Appendix A. However, their power lies in a more mysterious realm of sound and continuous linkage to the past and to the *source* of all consciousness and the vision of Zarathustra. The performance of the mathras causes a certain *resonance* with these sources and brings the individual living today into intimate contact with this source in a truly *magical* way.

In ritual and in the practice of prayer, verbal formulas are of two distinct types: *mathras* in Avestan and Pahlavi, and other components in English or the common language of the people. Typically the *mathras* are performed as a chant or song, and performed in a bold style, while the prayers in the common language are spoken in an undertone. The *mathras* carry the divine linkage and fulfill inner work, whereas the prayers in normal language give outer direction and can also express free personal wishes or promises. Remember that the Wise Lord is known to be a friend to individual humans and is willing and happy to help when asked.

Three Important *Mathras*

There are three important prayers or *mathras* which you should try to memorize in Avestan and recite from memory on a daily basis. The spelling given here approximates a phonetic representation of the sounds as easily understood by a speaker of modern English. These *mathras* are analyzed in greater detail in Appendix A.

Jasa me avanghe Mazda.

Ashem vohu vahishtem asti
ushta asti ushta ahmai
hyat ashai vahishtai ashem.

Yatha ahu vairyo atha ratush ashat chit hacha
vangeush dazda manango shyaothananem angeush Mazdai
khshathraremcha Ahurai a yim dregubyo dadat vastarem.

Any one or all three of these prayers can be recited before the open flame on your personal *khwan* as a regular and daily act of faithfulness and spiritual focus and direction. Each of the prayers should be repeated three times. Minimally this should be done once a day, but five times are ideal.

The Five *Gahs*

Zarathustra instituted the idea of praying several times a day at various stations of the sun's journey. By tradition there are five such times, called *gah* or "time for prayer." These five times link our consciousness to the natural cycle of the day, but more importantly these act as check-points for our own individual activities during the course of the day. They encourage us to think, say and do the right things to fulfill our goals and those of the Wise Lord, and they encourage us to make regular contact with the Lord to give us productivity, strength and awareness. These ideas, like so many others of the Prophet, were taken up by other religions and even self-help gurus over the millennia. We think they work best in the context they worked first.

In the beginning stages of taking up the practices of the Mazdan Way it is impractical to try to perform the *Gahs* in the manner of a pious orthodox Zoroastrian. Even among them there exists the tradition that instead of the usually prescribed prayers, one can recite sixty-five Ahunvars at each *Gah*. The use of prayer-beads (101 beads on a string) can be helpful in therese practices. Such prayer-beads were invented by Zoroastrians. From them it passed to Hindus, Christians and Muslims at later times. Zarathustra was said to have thwarted an assassination attempt when he threw his prayer-beads at the assailant, who dropped dead when struck by them. To begin with the Mazdan can pray once a day, then twice, then three times, eventually building up to the five *Gahs*. Begin with reciting the Ashem Vohu and the Ahunvar. Then begin to recite them multiple times each (in multiples of three). Pre-Zoroastrian Iranians (like other Indo-European peoples) held rites three times a day, at dawn, noon and sunset. Zarathustra added two more times:

Time	Name	Time-Span
Morning	Havan Gah	Sunrise to Noon
Noon	Rapithwan Gah	Noon to 3 p.m.
Afternoon	Urizan Gah	3 p.m. to Sunset
Sunset	Aiwisruthrem Gah	Sunset to Midnight
Night	Ushahen Gah	Midnight to Sunrise

The times for the performance of these prayer formulas can be flexible. A working person might do them upon rising, around noon, once in the afternoon, immediately after work and then at bed-time. It may be practical only to have presence of an open flame at home in the morning and in the evening. Any source of light is acceptable in less formal settings. Facing the visible sun is always a good alternative.

Chapter 12
Yearly Festivals, Celebrations and Rituals

The Holy Calendar

A detailed presentation of the complexities of the traditional eastern Zoroastrian religious calendar can be found at the website: www.heritageinstitute.com/zoroastrianism. Detailed knowledge of this calendar is not essential to following the Good Religion. All dates discussed here have been regularized to our conventional calendrical system. The benefit of knowledge of the traditional eastern calendar(s) is that, because each day is dedicated to a particular Archangel or angel, knowledge of this can help systematically and regularly focus and calibrate one's consciousness toward inner development. This was the sacred purpose of the calendar in the first place. Knowledge and use of this calendar is encouraged for more advanced development.

The Good Religion is one especially rich in festivals and celebrations. If a person loves parties, the Good Religion is a fitting home. There are two classes of these: seasonal festivals, called Gahambars and celebrations called Jashnes. The eastern Zoroastrian calendar does not have weeks as we know them. There are twelve solar months of thirty days each, each month and each day is dedicated to a spiritual entity. The months roughly begin in the middle of our conventional months, approximately corresponding to the time when the sun moves from one astrological sign to another. The Occidental Temple of the Wise Lord uses a synthesis of this system and our familiar Gregorgian Calendar. For the sake of simplicity and accuracy, we will discuss the holy days in terms of dates drawn from the Gregorgian Calendar. Organized Western Mazdan tradition has incorporated the week, the weekend and regular Sunday services into the sacred treatment of time.

The seven great seasonal celebrations in the Good Faith closely correspond to ritual seasonal calendars found in other Indo-European cultures. However, in our understanding they are also linked to the process of enacting and preserving the powers of the Seven Creations and the Bounteous Spirits. These consist of New Year and the six great and obligatory celebrations (*Gahambars*).

89

Festival	Date	Creation	Bounteous Spirit
1. New Year	March 21	Fire	Best Truth
2. Midspring	April 30	Sky	Sovereign Kingdom
3. Midsummer	June 29	Water	Perfection
4. Harvest	September 12	Earth	Holy Devotion
5. Herding-Time	October 12	Plants	Immortality
6. Midwinter	December 31	Cattle	Good Mind
7. Midpath	March 16	Man	Bounteous Spirit

Traditionally these celebrations went on for five days. We celebrate these on the nearest Saturday and Sunday following the date of the traditional beginning of the period, as given in the table above.

The first of these celebrations is the Mazdan New Year which centers on the spring Equinox. In some respects it holds the same kind of importance and meaning for followers of the Good Religion as does the Midwinter, or Yule-Tide for the Germanic tradition or Samhain for the Celts.

Here, as everywhere, we see the blending of the spiritual and abstract with the natural and down-to-earth. For the Good Religion these two are not separate, but grow out of and back into one another. They are linked in their Goodness (constructiveness, beauty, power and consciousness).

In what follows we will provide a home-based version of the ritual of celebration that can be used for each of these festivals. Members of the Temple may experience more elaborate versions, and ideally these are to be celebrated by an ordained priest at a fully functioning temple with the whole community participating in the joyous occasion. They are two-day affairs, with the first day spent in preparing for the ritual and feast to follow on the second day. The actual celebration consists of two major parts: 1) the ritual and 2) the feast (followed by the distribution of the remaining food to the poor and those in need).

These festivals are meant to be *enjoyed* by people. Good cheer and glad hearts should fill the participants.

BASIC HOUSEHOLD RITUAL FORMAT
FOR *GAHAMBAR*-FESTIVALS

We have already presented the basic ritual format of the simplest form of a group-ritual, and now it is time to delve into the particulars of how to perform each part of the rite:

0. Preparation of Ritual Objects and Space

All objects, tools and the area in which the ritual is to take place are to be carefully prepared and arranged for beginning the ceremony. Two celebrants, the *zaotar* (officiant) and *raspi* (assistant), are required for the correct completion of the ritual described here. Both are responsible for checking the correct arrangement of objects to be used. The diagrams below show the arrangement of the objects and the celebratory participants. Celebrants may either sit on the floor, sit in chairs, or stand. In each case the height of the ritual-table must be adjusted to accommodate the ease of the ritual activities. In each case the fire in the *afrinagan* should be just below eye-level of the official participants. The fire in the oil-lamp is to be lit by an assistant before the celebrants arrive before the altar-table. Ideally the ritual and the words spoken should be memorized. Printed words can be used as prompts by beginners.

1. Purification and Preparation of Active Celebrants

The active celebrants put on all-white clothing and a white cap or head-dress. They then wash their faces and hands, and rinse their mouths— all with pure, clean water. If they know the *kusti* rite and can perform it, they do so in private before the ritual begins.

2. Lighting of Fire

The celebrants come to the altar-table and take their respective places. The *raspi* takes fire from the *divo* and lights the fuel on the *afrinagan*. Once the fire is well tended and burning healthily, the *raspi* intones: *Yazdān ni Yād* ("In honor and to the glory of the Creator").

Then he places incense on the fire, and intones: *Nemase te Atarsh Mazdao* ("Homage to thee, O Fire of Wisdom").

3. Opening Prayers

The two celebrants both recite in unison the Ashem Vohu and the Ahunvar three times each. During these recitations the celebrants gaze steadily into Atar and forge the link with the divine realm of Ahura Mazda.

4. Recitations Purpose

Then follow four sections of words and actions meant to give direction and purpose the linkage that has been formed with the divine realm.

a) For the specific purpose of the festival:

These are recited in English, or the language of the country one lives in, in order to give conscious direction to the minds of the participants relevant to the time of the *Gahambar*.

1. New Year: In this the time of the New Day we honor and worship the Fire, that reflects the mind of the Wise Lord, and at this time we do also honor and worship Asha Vahishta, who is the Best Truth.
2. Midspring: In this the time of midspring we honor and worship the sky, that above us and of the wide realm of space, and at this time we do also honor and worship Khshathra Vairya, who is Sovereign Kingdom.
3. Midsummer: In this, the time of midsummer, we honor and worship the Waters of the sea, rivers and lakes and the rain which falls upon the earth, and at this time we do also honor and worship Haurvatat, who is Perfection.
4. Harvest: In this the Harvest time we honor and worship the earth, our planet and the soil, and at this time we do also honor and worship Spenta Armaiti, who is Holy Devotion.
5. Herding-Time: In this, the Herding-Time, we honor and worship the the plants of the world that grow wild and those we cultivate and at this time we do also honor and worship Ameretat, who is Immortality.
6. Midwinter: In this the Midwinter time we honor and worship the Soul of the Ox and all the beloved animals wild and domestic at this time we do also honor and worship Vohu Manah, the Good Mind.
7. Midpath: In this the time of the midpath in-between we honor and worship Mankind, the comrade and coworker of the Wise Lord, and at this time we do also honor and worship the Spenta Mainyu, who is the Bounteous Spirit.

b) For remembrance of the ancestors and heroes:

The *zaotar* intones *Ashō Farohar ni Yād* ("In honor of the dear departed holy ones") in the Avestan three times.

5. Consecration of Consumables and Exchange of Flowers

This section is really the core of the rite in that this is the culmination of the intersection between the heavenly and mundane realms. The spiritual power of the Wise Lord and the Archangels and angels is transferred to the food and drink on the altar table through the words and actions that are performed here:

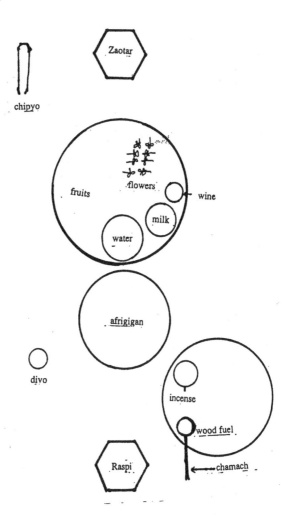

Diagram of Ritual Table/Altar

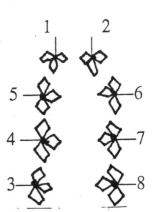

The Numerical Ordering of the Flowers for Ritual

The *zaotar* picks up the first two flowers while three *Ashem Vohus* are recited by both celebrants and he gives one of the flowers to the *raspi* at the end of the third *Ashem Vohu*. The *raspi* begins to recite the Khshnuman of Ahura Mazda and is joined by the *zaotar* on the word *"afrinami"* (I desire).

yasnemca vahmemca aojasca zavareca āfrīnāmi
ahurahe mazdā raēvatō hvarenanguhatō
("Worship and adoration and strength and force I desire
for Ahura Mazda, rich, possessing good things")

Upon the completion of this prayer an exchange of the first two flowers (1-2) takes place between the *zaotar* and the *raspi*. The two flowers represent the Spirit of God (Spenta Mainyu) in both the spiritual and physical worlds.

Both priests then begin to recite *Yasna 35*. (For an English version of this *Yasna* see Appendix B.) Upon the words *humatanam, hukhtanam, hvarshtanam* ("of good thoughts, good words and good actions"), the *zaotar* gives three flowers (3,4,5) to the *raspi*. This second verse is repeated once more and three more flowers are given to the *raspi*, this time from the lower left-hand column moving upwards (flowers 6,7,8).

At this point the *raspi* has eight flowers in his hand. Towards the end of the prayer (*Yasna 35.2*) the *raspi* transfers the ladle from his left to his right hand, being sure that the ladle is in contact with the *afrinagan*.

The *zaotar* holds the tongs in his right hand and touches it to the *afrinagan*, simultaneously touching the tray of fruits with his left hand. Both priests recite an *Ahunvar*. During this the *zaotar* touches four points on the circular water vessel with the tongs in an up-down, right-left motion as shown in diagram A.

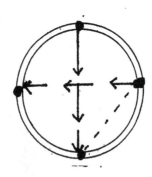

Diagram A: Motion of the First Touching the Four Points

94

He then touches the *afrinagan* to complete the circuit. Next he recites an *Ashem Vohu* during which touches the water pot at the four points in a circular clockwise direction, as shown in Diagram B.

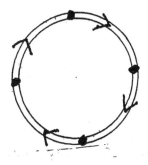

Diagram B: Motion of the Second Touching the Four Points

He then passes the tongs over the the fruit offerings after which he again touches the tongs to the *afrinagan*.

The *raspi* hands back the eight flowers to the *zaotar*. Both recite the *Ahunvar* twice, followed by the small *Khshnuman* of Ahura Mazda:

> *yasnemca vahmemca aojasca zavareca āfrīnāmi*
> *ahurahe mazdā raēvatō hvarenanguhatō*
> ("Worship and adoration and strength and force I desire
> for Ahura Mazda, rich, possessing good things")

Then conclude with one *Ashem Vohu*.

The ritual handshake known as the *hamazor* is done. While they quietly say to one another: *hamāzor hamā ashō bēt* ("May we all be one in Asha"). The *raspi* then performs the *hamzor* with a member of the congregation, who passes it on to others present.

Both priests begin to read or recite from Yasna 35.2 onwards to the end.

6. Solemn and Silent Consumption of Sacralized Food and Drink

Then there follows a solemn and silent consumption of a portion of the foods and drink that were consecrated on the *khwan* during the ritual. All persons present who wish to may take part in this magical feast. Silence it to be maintained throughout, although music can be played during this section. Only relatively small amounts of food and drink are consumed here. (All of the food must eventually be consumed by man or animal.)

95

7. Closing Formulas

In order that all who have actively participated in the *Gahambar* receive the blessings which have been invoked, all join hands in a ring around the fire and the celebrants intone the closing *mathra*: *hamāzor hamā ashō bēt*. Then the celebrants and the people all chant: *atha jamyāt yatha āfrināmi* ("Thus may it come as I wish").

A solitary version of this ritual is also available.

The Individual *Gahambars*

Each of the following descriptions of the *Gahambars* contains the basic information about the significance of the time in question. Each of these could be expanded greatly, however, these descriptions are sufficient to realize the core values of each.

1. New Year
Nowruz
March 21 (Spring Equinox)

This *Gahambar* festival is dedicated to Fire and to the Amesha Spenta named Asha Vahishta or "Best Truth." This is the most sacred time of year for Mazdans. The whole spring-time is a time of holiday festivities, akin to the way the fall is typically celebrated in the western Indo-European world. Ideally the New Year will be celebrated for a five day period. This festival was so powerful to the Iranian Zoroastrians that not even Islam could displace its importance. Nowruz is celebrated in Iran today with many pre- and non-Islamic characteristics, much as the Yule-tide is celebrated in Europe with many pagan elements, despite nominal Christianization. In both instances this shows the ingrained and innate power of the Indo-European cultural substratum. The tern *Nowruz* literally means "new day."

New Year is preceded by Chaharshambe Suri— Wednesday Feast, held on Tuesday night that comes before *Nowruz*. It is characterized by the building of seven small outdoor bonfires at sundown. During the night the gathered people have a party and take turns jumping over the fires chanting the Persian formula: *Sorkhie tu az man. Zardieh man az tu.*" ["Give me your ruddy complexion. Take my sickly pallor."] These fires are symbolic of the purifying fire as well as the mind of God.

The New Year is the recreation of the world. Although the overall cosmology of the Mazdan Religion seems to be linear in the sense that the world has a beginning, middle and end of time, from another perspective it demonstrates a great cycle. Each year is a small version of that cycle.

96

One of the most conspicuous features of the *Nowruz* celebration is the setting up of a *haft shin* table. This is still widely practiced in many nations that were once part of the ancient Persian Empires. *Haft shin* means "seven sh's." It is called this because the names of the seven things on the table are supposed to start with the letter *shin* in Persian. The names and symbols have been somewhat Islamicized in the mainstream version practiced in nominally Islamic countries today, but it is originally a Zarathustrian celebration and the old forms can still be found. Of course, the setting up of similar symbolic tables is common in many other festivals and celebrations of the Good Religion.

The seven elements of the table represent all the six Amesha Spentas plus Ahura Mazda, as well as the Seven Creations. They are:

1. *Sharab*: Wine
2. *Shakar*: Sugar
3. *Shir*: Milk
4. *Shireh*: Syrup
5. *Shahd*: Honey
6. *Shirini*: Candy
7. *Shir-berenj*: Rice-pudding

It should also contain the following items: a source of flame (candles or oil-lamp), white flowers, a dish of newly sprouted wheat or other grass and a portrait of the Prophet.

2. Midspring
Maidyozarem
April 30

The name of this celebration means mid-spring. It is generally the time when barley and wheat are harvested. Cosmologically the festival is focused on the Sky and on the archangel known as Khshathra Vairya, or "Sovereign Kingdom." As the Sky was mythically said to be made of metal, the element of metal is sacred to this time as well.

3. Midsummer
Maidyoshem
June 29

Here the name of the festival literally translates to "mid-summer," although it comes a bit later than the astronomical event itself. Agriculturally, it is the time when the summer crops rice and millet are sown. In cosmological symbolism this time is dedicated to Water, and to the archangel known as Haurvatat, or "Perfection."

4. Harvest
Paitishem
September 12

The literal meaning of the word is "harvesting time," and refers to the harvest of early growing summer crops and the hay for the cattle. The time is holy to the Earth and dedicated to the archangel called Spenta Armaiti, or "Holy Devotion."

5. Herding-Time
Ayathrem
October 12

The literal meaning of the name of the Gahambar is "herding-time" and refers to the archaic times when the herds were brought in from the pastures for the winter. It is also the time of preparation for sowing seed in the winter are made. The time is holy to the Plants and dedicated to the archangel Ameretat, or "Immortality."

6. Midwinter
Maidyarem
December 31

The mid-winter celebration is a time when the cattle and horses as well as the men and women had a time of rest and recreation. It is sacred to Cattle and dedicated to the archangel Vohu Manah, or "Good Mind."

7. Midpath
Hamaspathmaidyem
March 16

Here the literal meaning of the name of the celebration is "equal path in the middle" and refers the fact that the nights and days are in a time of approximate equality. There is neither excessive heat or cold. This is still a time of rest and recreation among the farmers and herders, but it is now a time also for prayer and spiritual recollection leading to the New Year. The time is holy to the creation called Man and dedicated to the archangel known as Spenta Mainyu, or the "Bounteous Spirit."

Name-Days and Other Festivals

In addition to the *Gahambars* there are numerous celebrations called Jashnes. Many of these are so-called name-days. The names of these celebrations generally end in the suffix *-gan*. Name-days occur in the Zoroastrian calendar when the name of the month coincides with the name of the day in that month, for example in the month of Fravardin the day name Fravardin both of which refer to the *fravashis* is a name-day. Many of these are celebrated at home by families and friends. They are also generally recognized in Temple-services on the Sunday following their dates.

Name	Date	Significance
Zarathustra's Birth	March 26	The Advent of the Good Religion
Easter	Various	The Saoshyants
Fravardigan	April 8	Fravashis
Ardibeheshtgan	April 22	Good-order and cleanliness
Khordadgan	May 25	Water
Tirgan	July 1	Settlement of Disputes, Freedom
Amordadgan	July 25	Plants and Vegetables
Shahrivargan	August 21	The Sky and Minerals
Mehergan	October 2	Friendship, loyalty and kindness
Abangan	October 26	Creation of the Waters
Azargan	November 24	Creation of Fire
Daegan	December 16	God as Creator
Yalda	December 21	Birth of Light
Christmas	December 25	Light in the North
Zarathustra's Death	December 26	Reflection on Mortality
Bahmangan	January 16	Animals
Sadeh	January 30	Discovery of Fire
Esfandegan	February 18	Earth-Creation
Purim	March 15	Respect for Diversity

These times for *Jashnes* should be observed privately in the home, and more formal times for get-togethers around the time of the festival can be arranged by fellow adherents of the Good Religion. These festivals are excellent to carry out, but they are not as obligatory as the *Gahambars*.

BASIC HOUSEHOLD RITUAL FORMAT
FOR FESTIVALS OR *JASHNES*

Although the *Gahambars* are the most sacred holidays in the Mazdan calendar, the lesser festivals are in many ways more intimate and family-oriented affairs. Whereas the *Gahambars* are most fittingly celebrated in a community center, such as a temple, the name-days and other festivals are just as rightly carried out in people's private homes. This makes them of extreme importance to this stage of development of the Good Religion in the West today.

The ritual for the celebration of these festivals follows a four-step procedure:

1) Arrangement of the *Khwan*
2) Lighting of the Fire
3) Gifts to the Fire
4) Festivities

The festivals are much less formal than the *Gahambars* as far as the actual ritual elements are concerned. They should be observed even by lone practitioners, but again are best celebrated in a group of fellow religionists.

Now let us present a description of these four steps, plus a fifth optional one:

1. Arrangement of the *Khwan*

We have already discussed the so-called *haft shin* or *haft chin* table connected to the celebration of Nowruz. Such symbolic tables are common in almost all festival celebrations. The (table) should be arranged with the symbolic elements needed or fitting for the specific festival in question. It should be set up at least a day or two prior to the beginning of the festival. Any perishables, such as fresh fruit or milk should only be added right before the festival begins. The (table) should be prominent in the environment of the celebration, but should not be in a place where it will be likely to be disturbed or accidentally damaged. For most festivals the (table) should be covered with a white cloth and decorated with some of the following items:

1) oil-lamp / *divo* or candles (fire)
2) dried fruits and nuts (problem solving)
3) fresh fruits (plants)
4) flowers (life)
5) portrait of Zarathustra (man)
6) unleavened bread / *dron* (consecration)
7) bowl of spring or rain water (water)
8) pomegranates (immortality)
9) painted eggs (humanity / fertility)
10) a mirror (sky/space)
11) sprays of cypress or pine (plants)
12) images of animals (animals)
13) sprouts of grass growing in a dish (plants)
14) apple (earth, beauty and health)
15) goldfish in a bowl (animals, movement and joy)
16) honey (animal / acquired wisdom)
17) milk (animal / innate wisdom)
18) a copy of the *Shahnama* or the *Avesta* (good words)
19) wine in a jug or glass (spirit / body)
20) stone (earth)

21) coins (metal, hope and prosperity)
22) metal bowls or dishes (metal)
23) orange floating in a crystal bowl (earth in space/water)
24) garlic (protection from evil)
25) vinegar (longevity and patience)
26) *malido*, a sweet almond/wheat pudding (sweetness of life)
27) sumac berries (new dawn)
28) dried oleaster fruit (love)
29) pictures of ancestors or heroes (ancestors and heroes)
30) watermelon (good luck)
31) *goshudo*, purified butter (animal productivity)
32) honey (sweetness of wisdom)
33) *sofreh* white cloth covering (sacred space)
34) raw dry rice grains (abundance)
35) coconut (inner and outer life)

Bowls should be made of wood, metal or earthenware. Some care should be taken to represent a balance of all of the Seven Creations in the symbolism of the arrangement. A minimum of seven items are used to adorn the table. It should be arranged in an artful and aesthetic fashion. The arrangement of the *khwan* is its own art-form.

A pedestal holding the *afrinagan* should be close by, and also similarly prominent, yet again protected from any accidental disturbance.

2. Lighting of the Fire

The designated celebrant should effectively arrange the fuel on the *afrinagan*, and take fire from the oil lamp (*divo*) on the *khwan* and light the fire of the *afrinagan* with the words: *Yazdān ni Yād* ("In honor and to the glory of the Creator").

This is followed by the recitation of the Ahunvar.

3. Gifts to the Fire

The lead celebrant makes the first a gift to Atar with words appropriate to the celebration. Thereafter each follower of the Good Religion present may make a gift of dry wood or incense to the Fire either silently or with some vocal formula.

The lead celebrant (or priest, if one is present) may make a short sermon on the meaning of the celebration and lead the Mazdans in the recitation of short prayers such as the Ashem Vohu and the Ahunvar.

4. Celebration

After the gifts of incense or wood have been given or sacrificed to Atar, there follows the general celebration which may contain festival-specific sub-rituals or customs. This may, on the other hand, simply have the general atmosphere of a joyous and happy party.

101

5. Group Performance of *Gahs* when Desired

During the course of the festival the various *gah*-prayer rituals may be conducted in a group format at the appropriate times of the day or evening (noon, mid-afternoon, and sunset).

The Annual *Jashnes*

This description of the annual Jashnes or festivals of the calendar serves as an introduction to the subject, but is, of course, in no way an exhaustive treatment of the meaning of these times. It will be noted that three festivals have been included from non-Zoroastrian tradition. Two of them from the Western Christian tradition, Christmas and Easter, and one from the Jewish calendar, Purim. These have been included for various reasons in the holy calendar of the Occidental Temple of the Wise Lord. Christmas, or Yule, has its origins in pagan European tradition, and is a festival that was so deeply ingrained in our culture that the Church could not displace it. Churchmen had to "Christianize" it as best they could. We reclaim this festival as an Indo-European feature. Easter (also to a lesser extent a Christianized version of a pagan festival) is a time of conscious outreach by the Mazdan Temple to the wider (at least nominally Christian) community around us. It is a time to teach about the Zoroastrian nature of the mission of Jesus to the Jews, and his role as a Saoshyant. Similarly the Jewish festival of Purim is a time of outreach to the Jewish community, and was chosen because the events it commemorates took place among the Persian Jews in ancient times and the festival itself has many Iranian characteristics.

Zarathustra's Birth
March 26
Khordad Sal

The actual date of Zarathustra's birth is unknown. The date upon which his birth is celebrated varies widely among followers of the eastern branch of the Good Religion. As one of the important aspects of this celebration is the idea of taking a personal inventory of one's life, past performance and future plans. It seems correct that it should come in conjunction with the time of our New Year. Hence the date of March 26 seems most fitting. The celebration is a joyous one with a birth-day-party-type atmosphere.

Easter

This is, of course, not a festival of the eastern orthodox Zoroastrian religion. In the Temple of the Wise Lord it is celebrated on the conventional date of Easter in your own community. In the West this has been calculated as the first Sunday after the first full moon after the spring equinox. For us this day recognizes the role of the external

102

mission of the Zoroastrians of ancient times to interact with all peoples of the world and their recognition of the validity of other paths, while maintaining at the same time the *best truth* represented by the Mazdan Revelation of Zarathustra. Here we recognize Jesus the Nazarene as a foreign Saoshyant, his martyrdom at the hands of the Romans, and the account of his bodily resurrection as a demonstration of the power of the Wise Lord. This day is also one of outreach to professing Christians.

Fravardigan
April 8
This is a celebration of the *fravashis*. These are the "guardian angles" of individuals. But that may be misleading to some. They are not entities separate from individuals, but rather are their higher or spiritual selves which pre-existed our incarnation. This is the part of us which made the choice to come to earth and enter the battle against the forces of destruction and chaos. This is a time to reflect on the fact that we have made that choice, to remember that choice and to recall who we really are on this earth. It is a time to become resolute and give a good direction to life. The *fravashi* exists in three states: 1) the *fravashi* of the unborn, 2) of the living and 3) of the dead. This is a time to honor and worship the *fravashis* of the dead, especially those of our own families. These are especially close to us at this time. Offerings of fruit, incense, flowers wood and money are made to the *fravashis* at the fire-altar.

Ardibeheshtgan
April 22
This is the Festival of Flowers. It is dedicated to Asha Vahishta and celebrates good order, cleanliness and truth. It is a flower-festival, as flowers are in full bloom at this time. Celebrants dress all in white and enjoy the spring time. It is a good day to work in the garden with full awareness and consciousness of the meaning of the work done there. This has become an important festival in the Netherlands.

Hordadgan
May 25
Here we have Festival of the Waters and of Drink. It is dedicated to Haurvatat and celebrates the life-giving power of water— rivers, lakes, the sea and ocean. Haurvatat stands for Perfection and Wholeness. Prayers and meditations should be done in the presence of water.

Tiregan
July 1
This festival commemorates the ancient truce between the warring camps of Iran and Turan. Both sides were weary of war and beset by

drought. The name of the festival refers to the name Tir (arrow) and/or Tishtar (lightning bolt/the Star Sirius). When the two warring factions decided to make peace, it was necessary to establish a border betwen them. The archer Arash was to loose his mighty arrow, and where it landed would be the border between them. The arrow was loosed at dawn and flew until noon. This made the area of Iran to enclose the area of Turan. The arrow also caused a great thunderstorm, releasing the pent-up waters from the sky, ending the drought with rain falling on the lands of Iran and Turan together. The festival is one of diversity and peace between peoples. It is a custom for people to wear rainbow colored wristbands (sometimes with bands containing prayers written out by priests). These are worn for ten days, and then disposed of in running water. The Tirgan Festival is a large Iranian cultural festival held in Toronto, Canada in July.

Amordadgan
July 25
This festival day is dedicated to the spirit of Immortality (Ameretat) and to the natural phenomena protected by that spirit, that is, plants and vegetables and food in general. This is a celebration of long and healthy life and the immortality of the soul. In old Zoroastrian culture food was taken in silence out of respect for Ameretat, so that this spirit would not be sullied with idle chatter.

Shahrivargan
August 21
Here we have a festival dedicated to Khshathra Vairya — Desirable Sovereignty — who is the protector of the Sky and of Minerals. This is observed as a recognition of fathers, and so is our Fathers' Day. It is a day characterized by outdoor parties and cookouts where kabobs are roasted on open fires. But more importantly it is a time for the recognition that good government in the world is one that is the choice of the people, a principle founded by Zarathustra in the Gatha (16):

> The good dominion is to be chosen.
> It is the best dividend.
> In fact, it is devotion for the dedicated,
> who, Wise One, moves best
> within righteousness by his deeds.
> It is for this dominion that I am working for all of us now.

This is a day to spend time helping the poor and the oppressed, wherever they are to be found, and working toward Good Dominion.

Mehrgan
October 2

This is the Festival of Autumn dedicated to Mithra (Mehr). Some of the ancients thought of this time as a "new year." Legend has it that the hero Fereydun vanquished the evil Dahak on this day. Dahak had previously killed Jamshid, who had established Nowruz as the New Year. Here we see a polarity between Spring and Autumn. This festival was celebrated lavishly in Persepolis in ancient times. It was the time when representatives from throughout the empire came to pay their taxes to the "King of Kings." It is a time of gift-giving. In ancient times everyone gave gifts to the emperor, each according to his or her financial abilities. Records of these gifts were kept. If at a future time a person fell on hard times and had need, their gifts would be returned to them times two. During this festival the emperor wore a fur robe, and gave away all of his summer clothes to the people. In the present day Mehrgan is occasion for a party with a lavishly set table with the usual items. A special addition is a mirror and some eyeliner. (Traditionally this is kohl or *sorme* in Persian. It is now illegal to import this into the USA because it contains lead.) The celebration begins at lunch-time. At one point the participants stand before the mirror for prayers, drink a glass of sharbat (a beverage prepared from fruit or flower petals) and then have the eyeliner applied to their eyes and look at themselves in the mirror. This has the effect of a prayer for good fortune and it is a way to drive away negative forces.

Abangan
October 26

This is the Festival of Waters. It is sacred to the old Iranian goddess Anahita— the "spotless" or "undefiled." The main religious activity done in this celebration is the recitation of the "Homage unto Waters" prayer in the presence of water.

Azargan
November 24

This is the Fire Festival name-day in which the Atash is honored with a private home-gathering and party. Fragrant woods and incense are offered to the fire in the home *afrinagan* (fire-vase) by participants. Preferred woods are sandalwood or juniper.

Daegan
December 16

This is the Festival of the Creator-God. The Wise Lord is honored as the Creator (Dadvah) of the World and all of the good creations, material and spiritual.

Yalda
December 21

The similarities between the significance and the rituals surrounding this celebration have led some to believe that our European Christmas customs were derived from Persia! Of course, the answer to the similarities is to be found in the common Indo-European roots of both and in the fact that our Germanic traditions have a special close affinity with Iranian ones due to the ancient connections between our peoples. It is perhaps more than mere coincidence that the three *magavans* are mentioned in the story of the birth of Jesus. Historians of Christian church practices can tell you that in the beginning of organized Christianity, Christmas was not observed or celebrated. It was only when Germanic peoples began to be Christianized that the celebration became important. At first it was called the "Gothic celebration."

In the Good Religion, Yalda celebrates the Birth of the Light. Yalda means "birth." The *yazata* Mithra is born on the morning after the long night of Yalda. The celebration is dedicated to Mithra. It was due to miscalculations in ancient times that the Birth of Mithras was moved from December 21 to December 25, and the Christian church placed the birth of Jesus on that date to try to co-opt the importance of the day from the Romans and others practicing Mithraism at the time. It was the custom to gather in caves in the mountains and stay up all night to greet the sun in the morning. Mithra is said to have been born "in a cave," because Iranian myth holds that the vault of heaven is made of "stone," and the light of the stars is a manifestation of the light of Mithra. (Again the birthplace of Jesus is said to be in a cave.) To practice Yalda today, we stay up all night and gather around the *korsi* (ritual table) which is adorned with flowers, lit candles, fruit (pomegranate and watermelon) along with nuts of various kinds. We eat food of this kind and listen to stories of the gods and heroes. It is considered good luck for the coming summer to eat watermelon on this night. This is a festival of light. Fires are kept burning all night and it is held to be the night when the light defeats the darkness of Ahriman.

Christmas / Yule
December 25

In the ancient cultures of northwestern Europe, late December had always been the most sacred time of the year. It continues to be so, even if in Christian guise. Here the birth of Jesus is celebrated. Originally it was the birth-date of Mithras. According to Christian mythology the infant Jesus was visited by three Zoroastrian priests (Magus) who honored him, recognized him and gave him gifts of gold, frankincense and myrrh. The time of year is also known in ancient northern Europe as Yule. Christians later made this a sacred time in their calendar to accommodate the people who were going to celebrate at this time regardless of the imposed new religion. We are now returning the favor. Normal family-based Christmas customs can be observed. The fire should receive the gifts of frankincense and myrrh, and the *khwan* should be decorated with a Nativity Scene which includes the "Three Wise Men."

Zarathustra's Death
Zartosht No-Diso
December 26

This is a commemoration of the life and death of the Prophet Zarathustra. It is a somber and serious time with lectures and prayers. Where fire-temples are present they are especially visited at this time.

Bahmangan
January 16

Here the Festival dedicated to Vohu Manah is celebrated. It is a day dedicated to the creation of the animals. On this day the animals of the community and the world are blessed and activities celebrating the material and spiritual contributions of animals to our lives are recognized. Throw a party for your pets. Refrain from eating meat.

Sadeh
January 30

This is a celebration of the Discovery of Fire and comes one hundred (*sadeh*) days/nights before the Spring Equinox, or New-Day. It is a recognition of the presence of the sacred fire within each of the creatures of God. The fire drives out the cold and drives away the forces of darkness.

Firdowsi in the *Shahnama* recounts how King Hushang, while in the mountains with his men, confronted a "world-consuming snake" and hurled a stone at it. The snake escaped but the stone hit the mountain with such force that sparks flew out "from their stony hiding place" and caught some brush on fire. It warmed the men and Hushang thanked God and told his men to consider the fire sacred and they held a feast to honor it.

A bonfire is lit and people gather around it, holding hands and praying to God for good fortune, fellowship and solidarity. The fire is kept burning all night and there is generally a festive mood and much good cheer. More modestly, a fire can be built indoors in a proper vase or urn (*afrinagan*) and similar activities ensue. This festival, like Nowruz and Yalda are national symbols of Iranian culture, regardless of the religion one professes.

107

Esfandegan

February 18

This celebration is also called Sepandarmazgan, a day dedicated to the Bounteous Spirit Armaiti (Devotion), protector of the Earth. (This archangel also has a Festival on September 12.) In this case, however, this is a so-called name-feast for Armaiti. It is a women's day. Men are supposed to lavish them with gifts and honor them. Armaiti is a protector of women. The day is one and the same with an agricultural festival when people pray for good harvests and to drive away evil spirits which might be intent on destroying the crops. Those familiar with comparative religion and folklore will recognize this as corresponding to European Valentine's Day and the pre-Lenten festivals such as Carnival or Fasching. The festival has been re-emphasized in modern Iran as a counter to European Valentine's Day.

Purim

March 15

The Jewish festival of Purim centers on historical events in Persia when the sizable Jewish population in the empire was threatened by overzealous and intolerant Magian priests and ministers, chief among them one known to Jewish legend as Haman. The Shah married a Jewish woman and with her influence the plot to destroy the Jews was reversed. Purim is celebrated by the Jews at various dates in the spring, and was apparently originally linked to Persian Nowruz festivities. Jewish lore records the events in the Book of Esther. For the Occidental Temple of the Wise Lord it is a day of outreach to the Jewish community and a day to celebrate the spirit of religious diversity and mutual respect. A study of the Jewish customs surrounding Purim indicates many Persian elements. It is a time of parties, masquerades and gift-giving— especially of food and wine.

Afterword:
The Occidental Temple of the Wise Lord

The Occidental Temple of the Wise Lord was founded on March 21, 2014 after many years of inner development. It is an entirely independent Western form of the Good Religion with Zarathustra as its Prophet. It is open to all and is truly the universal religion of all mankind as it is focuses on the one thing that all humans have in common— consciousness.

The purpose of the Temple is to establish an institutional base for the invigoration of the battle of the Wise Lord against the forces of ignorance, weakness and poverty within the human mind and in the world at large. With the clear message of the practice of Good Thought, Good Words and Good Actions, the Occidental Temple of the Wise Lord can and will open a new front in the struggle of the human spirit and of the Wise Lord against negative and destructive influences in the world. The message of Zarathustra, delivered almost four thousand years ago, is a call to human action. It is rooted in the same cultural soil as are the ancestral cultures of Europe but is the first philosophical and universal formulation of this great tradition. Unfortunately, although we have all heard of "magic," no one in the West has yet articulated the pure message of the Prophet of the Magians in a way that is clear and lucid.

Our vision is an expansive and vigorous one. The Good Religion is virile and dynamic, focused on inner development of the individual and immediate action in the world in harmony with the levels of development the individual has attained.

The basic goals of the Occidental Temple of the Wise Lord are:
- to develop a system of individual spiritual growth
- to articulate the Good Religion to a worldwide community
- to build Temples worldwide dedicated to the Good Religion
- to serve the interests of the Wise Lord in practical ways in the fight against destructiveness, disorder, ignorance, weakness and disease

Our goals are nothing short of world-transformation and the ushering in of the beginning stages of the "Making-Wonderful," the renovation of the world according to the mystery and logic of the Zarathustrian vision.

On the one hand we have the oldest history of any organized religion, as we are rooted in the Indo-European tradition and specifically in the Zarathustrian philosophy and theology, but on the other hand we are virtually without a history, a blank slate awaiting our story to be written. We are the newest and the oldest religion in the the world.

It is as if there had been a secret barrier preventing what seems to be the most obvious development from taking place. That development should have been the pure articulation of the Zarathustrian message in a Westernized form. Somehow at this time this barrier has now been breached; the Gate has been opened. A new beginning has been made possible. The blank slate is now ready to receive the inscriptions of history. May we be worthy of the joyous task at hand!

The structure of the entire organization is one governed by a High Priest assisted by a six member council. The main function of this group is the development and dissemination of information and the training and ordination of priests and priestesses. The real structure of the organization is contained in the local Temples (permanent establishments which maintain a Holy Fire, or Atar) and the local assemblies. This latter type of group is one that has no clergy to lead it, but which have an established place to meet and hold assemblies for worship and learning.

The point of our efforts is to accelerate and focus the performance of Good Thoughts, Good Words and Good Actions among human beings and to do so in a conscious way enriched by the tradition which gave rise to this philosophy. Our purpose is not to control or claim to monopolize anything. All people who practice the Good are *de facto* Mazdans— whether they call themselves Christians, pagans, Muslims, Jews, Hindus or Satanists. Many thinking persons have wondered at the plurality of religions in the world and pondered: "They can't all be right, or wrong." Furthermore it seems ludicrous to say that a good person, who just happens to follow a religion different from one's own, should be thought to be damned to hell because he is in the "wrong religion." The Mazdan Way sweeps all of this nonsense away. All people, regardless of what religion they profess, who practice Good Thoughts, Good Words and Good Actions in a conscious way, are in reality Mazdans. These will be rewarded for their work. Those who do not practice the Truth will not be rewarded, regardless of the religion they *profess*. I have known professing Satanists who were in fact saints, and Christian ministers who were *daevas* incarnate. The latter case is all too common because actual evil will always seek to hide itself in conventional symbols of "good."

The first phase of development for the OTWL involves the development of our teachings in a way that is intelligible to the Western world and to establish a network of individuals dedicated to the success of the Temple. Members of this network can include members and leaders of the orthodox Zoroastrian religion, from whom we also wish to learn. The second phase of development is one of expansion and establishment on local levels everywhere in the Western world. The final phase involves the development and establishment of a true priesthood—from which all good things will flow.

It should be recognized that the specific doctrines and rituals of the OTWL will remain flexible. We should guard against too quickly establishing hard-and-fast dogmas. Our general principles are clear, age-old and eternal. The methods of practicing these principles must remain open to the spirit of evolutionary creativity. Other "religions" have focused on minute dogmatic criteria which have little to do with the spirit of the quest— and have made themselves appear foolish in the eyes of thinking people everywhere.

In order to establish the Occidental Temple of the Wise Lord, we need to first set up a general international base of enthusiastic and knowledgeable members. This level of establishment is only a provisional one. Immediate action must then be taken to establish local Temples and assemblies.

Those who have studied, experienced and understood the principles of Mazdan creative evolution will recognize in this plan of development the ideas of abstract prototypes (*menog*) being actualized in materialized forms (*getig*).

Mazdans deal in reality — spiritual or material — not conventionality. The latter is the product of the ill-informed imaginings of the unthinking masses. It is no small part of the Mazdan mission in the world today to re-focus this philosophy within other religions. Our highest purpose is, however, to practice the philosophy in a pure and culturally intelligible form for the average Westerner. As practically no religion in the world is historically untouched by Indo-European and/or Zarathustrian ideas, beliefs or practices, the interaction between the Mazdan Way and other religions should be a friendly, non-confrontational one.

At this point in time there is much work that need to be done. We need a website, a regularly edited and produced newsletter, serious work on the development of a training curriculum for clergy and expertise in the conducting of local religious organizations. The spiritual prototype has been cast in the text of the book you now hold, the work of putting these spiritual principles into material manifestation lies before us. By implementing these ideas the fight will be taken directly to the forces of Ahriman, and the days of renewal will be brought ever closer by our efforts.

Seminary Work

We would like to form a seminary for the education of a clergy. At present we are in a pioneering phase. The next phase will deepen the cultural richness of the system and priests and priestesses will be educated in the following fields:

Doctrine of the Occidental Temple of the Wise Lord
Indo-European history, culture and religion
Iranian history, culture and religion
  Iranian Influence on other religions and cultures
  Study of one's own native tradition (e.g. Germanic, Celtic, Italic,
    Slavic, Chinese, African, Judaic)
Old Iranian languages:
  Avestan
  Old Persian
  Pahlavi
Modern Persian
History and teachings of the Zoroastrian religion
Ritual proficiency
Inner personal development
Pastoral care and counseling

We seek not only students in these fields but teachers as well.

The ultimate dream of the OTWL is to have hundreds and thousands of local Temples or churches throughout the Western world. Individuals now with no religion, as well as Christians, Jews, and professing pagans of various Indo-European cultural groups will turn to the Occidental Temple of the Wise Lord as the first and best expression of what religion can and should be. As opposed to some made-up doctrine, the Good Religion offers the best and oldest tradition of organized universal religion. It represents a return to the fountainhead of all religion and thus offers the hope of something to which all people, and all peoples, can turn. As the source of all religion, the philosophical and theological message of the Prophet Zarathustra can be the ultimate home for the human spirit, finally awakened to its true nature and purpose as a necessary comrade and co-worker with the Wise Lord for the perfection of the world.

Although the teaching of the Good Religion is universal, part of its absolute universality is the clear recognition that each individual is unique and authentic. Each individual has a separate heavenly proto-type *(fravashi)* — a virtual demigod/dess — which it is the living individual's task to actualize and realize. The reality of this philosophy is reflected in the practical recognition that each individual will have his or her own individual path to follow. Spiritual development is not measured in the level of conformity to the dogmas but in the optimal level of quality of an individual's thoughts, words and actions.

The OTWL is a *world-engaged* religion. Personal transformation is to be instantly translated into practical action in the world. No one can tell you what those actions will be, or "should" be, but anyone who has knowledge of the Truth *(Asha)* can see this quality in your actions at once. Each person will have his or her own pathway of action, but it is essential for the mission of the Wise Lord to be completed that all those who embrace the philosophy of the Good Religion band together to form a united front against the forces of destruction, disorder, ignorance, weakness, poverty and sickness. The formation of this united front is the ultimate dream of the Occidental Temple, a dream born of the eternal mandate of the Wise Lord.

Appendix A:
The Analysis of Three Major Avestan *Mathras*

Matras in the old Gathic dialect of Zarathustra are often almost impossible to translate. Their use of words and grammatical forms take on complex and multileveled meanings, and can sometimes seem to mean different things at different times. They are first and foremost holy words of power. Effort should, however, be made to understand the meaning of the words and to feel their meaning as much as possible during recitations of the formulas. With this in mind, these discussions are offered.

Jasa me Avanghe Mazda

jasa	*mē*	*avaŋhe*	*Mazdā*
come	to my	aid	Mazda (wisdom/God)

Translation:
Come to my aid, O Mazda!

Commentary:
This is the beginning of a longer *mathra*, but can be used alone in times of need. It can be as much a call to the right and proper organization of one's own mind or consciousness as it is a call to an outside entity, i.e. Ahura Mazda.

This *mathra* written in the *Din Dabireh* alphabet appears:

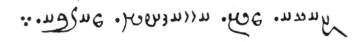

Ashem Vohu

ašem	*vohū*	*vahištem*	*astī*
asha	good	best	is

uštā	*astī*	*utšā*	*ahmāi*
happiness	is	happiness	for the one

hyat	*ašāi*		*vahištāi*	*ašem*
who (is)	for the sake of *asha*		the best	asha

115

Here is an approximate "translation" of the Ashem Vohu:
True order is the best good, and it is happiness. Happiness for the one
who is truly ordered for the sake of the best true order.

The overriding message of the *mathra* is that *asha* is the highest good
and that to attain happiness one must do the good for the sake of the
good order alone.

Here is the *Ashem Vohu* written in the *Din Dabireh* alphabet:

Ahunvar

Yaθa	*ahū*	*vairyō*		
Just as	a king	acts according to his will		

aθa	*ratuš*	*ašat*	*cit*	*haca*
so	the priest	true order	and other things	by means

vangeuš	*dazdā*	*manangō*
of good	the gift	mind

šyaoθananem	*anghēuš*	*Mazdai*
is for those working	of this world	for Mazda (wisdom)

xšaθraremca	*Ahurai*	*ā*
(accepts) the sovereign rule	of the Lord	as

yim	*dregubyō*	*dadat*	*vāstārem.*
he who	of the poor	constitutes himself	as protector

Here are two different "translations" of the Ahunvar:

Just as the king acts according to his will, so does the priest, by means
of true order, and so on, act according to his own will. The gift of the
good mind is for those working for Mazda in this world, he who

116

constitutes himself as the protector of the poor (accepts) the sovereign rule (of the entire world) (as it were) of the lord (Ahura).

As judgment is to be chosen by the world,
   so the judgment (which is) in accord with the truth,
(which is to be passed) on the actions of good throughout the world,
   is assigned to the Wise (Lord) [*Mazdai*],
and the power (is assigned) to the (Wise) Lord [*ahurai*]
   whom they established as a pastor to the needy.

Here is the Ahunvar written in the *Din Dabireh* alphabet:

Appendix B
YASNA 35
Praise to Ahura Mazda and the Immortals

1. We sacrifice to Ahura Mazda, the holy Lord of the ritual order, and to the Bountiful Immortals, who rule aright, who dispose of all aright; and we sacrifice to the entire creation of the pure, the spiritual and the physical, with the longing blessing of the beneficent ritual, with the longing blessing of the Good Religion, the Mazdan Faith.

2. We are the praisers of good thoughts, of good words, and of good actions, of those now and those hereafter of those being done now; and of those already completed. We implant them with our homage, and we do this all the more, and yet the more since we are praisers of the good from which they spring.

3. That, therefore, would we choose, O Ahura Mazda and thou, O Righteousness the beauteous that we should think, and speak, and do those thoughts, and words, and deeds, among actual good thoughts, and words, and actions, which are the best for both the worlds;

(4) and together with these gifts and actions which are thus the best, we would pray for the Kine which represents the pure creation, that she may have comfort and have fodder from the well-famed! and from the humble, from the powerful and the weak.

5. To the best of good rulers belongs indeed the Kingdom, because we render and ascribe it to Him, and make it thoroughly His own, to Mazda Ahura do we ascribe it, and to the Best Order.

6. As thus both man and woman know their duty, both thoroughly and truly, so let him, or her, declare it and fulfill it, and teach it to those who may perform it as it is.

7. We would be deeply mindful of Your sacrifice and homage, Yours, O Ahura Mazda! and the best, (and we would be mindful) of the nurture of the Kine. And that let us teach, and perform for You according as we may; and for those who praise you as we do.

8. Under the shelter of the ritual Order let us do so in the active fulfillment of its precepts toward every one of the pure and better creatures which are beneficial to life, with a gift for both the worlds.

9. Yea, those words and sayings, O Ahura Mazda we would proclaim as Right-Order, and as belonging to the Better Mind; and we would make Thee the one who both supports us in our proclamation of them, and who throws still further light upon them as they exist,

10. And by reason of Thy Right-Order, Thy Good Mind, and Thy Sovereign Power, and through the instrumentality of our praises of Thee, O Ahura Mazda, and for the purpose of still further praises, by Thy spoken words, and for still further spoken words, through Thy worship, and for still further forms of worship would we thus proclaim them, and make Thee the bestower of our light.

Resources

Many resources appear on the Internet for the study of material of vital interest to students of Mazdan spiritual traditions. These range from orthodox Zoroastrianism to the languages and texts needed for the in-depth study and understanding of Mazdan religion and spirituality. This is only a partial list of such resources.

There are several resources on the Internet for orthodox eastern Zoroastrianism. These contain many insights and information which are of great use to followers of the Good Religion in the West.

General

A tremendous collection of resources including texts and linguistic information is to be found at:
www.avesta.org

A comprehensive presentation of Zoroastrian heritage, which includes history, religion, rituals, calendar, and so on, is presented by author K. E. Eduljee at:
www.heritageinstitute/zoroastrianism

The Circle of Ancient Iranian Studies has a website dedicated to the "understanding and appreciation of pre-Islamic Iranian heritage."
www.cais-soas.com

Translations of Sacred Texts

Older translations of the most important Zoroastrian texts are available online at:
www.sacred-texts.com/zor/index.htm

These are the three volumes of the Avesta and five volumes of Pahlavi texts published in the Sacred Books of the East series.

Languages

For those interested in the original languages used in Zoroastrian texts, Avestan and Pahlavi, there are excellent, often downloadable, online lessons and grammars of these languages.

For the study of Pahlavi as a *living* language:
www.parsig.org

The Agha Khan Professor of Iranian, Oktar Prods Skjærvø, at Harvard University has produced a series of textbooks for the study of

Old Iranian languages:

Old Persian:
www.fas.harvard.edu/~iranian/Old Persian

Avestan:
www.fas.harvard.edu/~iranian/Avesta/avestancomplete.pdf

Old Avestan or Gathic
www.fas.harvard.edu/~iranian/Oldvestan/index.html

Bibliography

Boyce, Mary. *Zoroastrians: Their Religious Beliefs and Practices*. London: Routledge & Kegan Paul, 1986.

——————. *Textual Sources for the Study of Zoroastrianism*. Chicago: University of Chicago Press, 1984.

Clark, Peter. *Zoroastrianism*. Eastbourne: Sussex Academic Press, 1998.

Curtis, Vesta Sarkhosh. *Persian Myths*. Austin: University of Texas Press, 1993.

Ferdowsi. *The Epic of the Kings: Shāhnāma*. Trans. Reuben Levy. Chicago: University of Chicago Press, 1967.

Foltz, Richard C. *Spirituality in the Land of the Noble: How Iran Shaped the World's Religions*. Oxford: One World, 2004.

Frye, Richard N. *The Heritage of Persia*. New York: Mentor, 1966.

——————. *The Golden Age of Persia*. New York: Barnes and Noble, [1975].

Haug, Martin. *The Parsis: Essays on their Sacred Language, Writings and Religion*. New Delhi: Cosmo, [1978].

Hinnels, John R. *Persian Mythology*. London: Hamlyn, 1973.

Hovannisian, Richard G. and George Sabagh, eds. *The Persian Presence in the Islamic Word*. Cambridge: Cambridge University Press, 1998.

Kriwaczek, Paul. *In Search of Zarathustra*. New York: Knopf, 2003.

Malandra, William W., ed. tr. *An Introduction to Ancient Iranian Religion*. Minneapolis: University of Minnesota Press, 1983.

Mehta, K. P. *Our Heritage: Past and Present*. Bombay: P. N. Mehta Education Trust, [n.d.].

Mistree, Khojeste P. *Zoroastrianism: An Ethnic Perspective*. Bombay: Good Impressions, 1982.

Modi, J. J. *The Religious Ceremonies and Customs of the Parsees*. Bombay: J. B. Karani's Sons, 1937, 2nd ed.

Puhvel, Jaan. *Comparative Mythology*. Baltimore: Johns Hopkins University Press, 1987.

Rice, Tamara Talbot. *The Scythians*. London: Thames and Hudson, 1957.

Widengren, Geo. *Die Religionen Irans*. Stuttgart: Kohlhammer, 1965.

Zaehner, R. C. *The Dawn and Twilight of Zoroastrianism*. Phoenix Press: London, [1961].

——————. *Teachings of the Magi*. Oxford: Oxford University Press, 1976.

Glossary

afrinagan: (1) a multi-part ceremony of blessing, (2) the prayers recited during that ceremony, and (3) the vessel in which the sacred fire is tended.

Ahunvar: Name of the holiest prayer or *mathra* of the Mazdan faith, it begins with the phrase *"yatha ahu vairyo..."*

Asha: A basic concept of the Good Religion. There is no adequate English translation. It connotes a synthesis of world-order, truth, right, righteousness and holiness. Compare to Sanskrit *rita*.

Ashem Vohu: One of the most sacred mathras which praises Asha, and begins, *"ashem vohu..."*

Wise Lord: See Ahura Mazda.

Ahura Mazda: Literally "lord wisdom," more conventionally "the Wise Lord," and philosophically the principle of focused consciousness or *wisdom*. This is the one and true godhead of all humanity, first recognized as the universal divinity by Zarathustra though his insight (*daena*).

alat: Array of consecrated ceremonial implements used in a specific ritual.

Amesha Spentas: Avestan for "Immortal Bounteous Ones" and is the title of the six archangelic beings created by Ahura Mazda (see Yasna 47.1) to effect creation.

Atash: Consecrated Fire.

Aryan: A term for Indo-Europeans, especially in the eastern realms. The prefix Ar- is reflected in Persian Er- or Ir-, as in Ir-an. It is not a racial, but a religious term denoting those who worship the Aryan (Indo-European) gods and goddesses. Zoroastrians also attached themselves to the term.

Atar (Av.), (Phl.) Adar: (1) The consecrated fire. (2) The *yazata* of Fire.

Avesta: Holy scripture of the Mazdan religion.

Avestan: The archaic Indo-European language in which the earliest scripture is recorded. It is similar in structure to Rig Vedic Sanskrit.

daena: (1) Religion, (2) conscience, insight, inner consciousness of self, (3) a part of the soul which stores the faculty of insight or self-awareness.

daeva: A demon, or pattern of destructive or ignorant thought or action, in the inner or outer worlds.

Fravashi: Often referred to as a "guardian angel," the *fravashi* is the heavenly archetype of the individual soul. It is that part of humanity that actually chose to take up the struggle of the Wise Lord against the forces of destruction.

gah: (1) One of the five watches or times of the day when practitioners of the Good Religion pray, (2) a place or area for religious activities.

Gahambar: One of the major seasonal celebrations usually celebrated communally. There are six major *Gahambars* in addition to Nowruz.

Gathas: The 17 hymns composed by Zarathustra himself which are contained in the *Avesta*. They are in the most archaic dialect of Avestan, and date from around 1700 BCE.

getig: The world, material existence.

haoma: Ritual consecrated drink consumed in rites of the Good Religion. Compare to Sanskrit *soma*.

Indo-European: Academic term for the common ancestral culture and language which is the point of origin for most of the European cultures as well as those of the Iranian peoples and those of northern India. The more Romantic and perhaps antiquated term "Aryan" can be considered an equivalent.

Jashne: A celebration and ritual of blessing and thanksgiving conducted during festivals such as the *Gahambars*.

khwan: 1) A ritual table or altar. 2) Stone slab table used for rituals which stands on four feet.

khwarr: Avestan *khvarenah*, Pahlavi *khwarrah*, this word denotes the "glory" of an individual. It is the divine empowerment and/or luck attached to an individual. It is increased by ethical and heroic action. This is depicted in Iranian art as a nimbus, and is the origin of the "halo" in Western depictions of religious figures.

Magian: A popular term denoting priests and followers of the Zoroastrian religion especially in the western part of the Persian Empire.

mathra: Holy Word, many passages in the *Avesta* with specific spiritual qualities. These are verbal formulas which link the human and divine minds. Compare to Sanskrit *mantra*.

Mazdan: (1) Noun. A follower of the Good Religion in the new tradition of the Occidental Temple of the Wise Lord. (2) Adjective. Pertaining to the religion of the Wise Lord.

menog: The spiritual world and the prototype of the material world.

Saoshyant: A (World) Savior, one who has incarnated to bring and teach a new level of salvation to mankind. There are to be several of these throughout history, culminating in the final Saoshyant who will usher in the "Making Wonderful," or final Renovation.

topi: a white cap worn during prayers and rituals.

Truth: See *Asha*.

Yashts: These are 21 hymns in Younger Avestan which praise and invoke specific divinities or concepts.

Yasnas: Avestan texts arranged in 72 chapters which are recited in the ritual of Zoroastrianism, also called a *yasna*, or "worship." The Gathas are embedded in the Yasna texts. Most of them are in the slightly older dialect of the Avestan language.

yazata (Av.): Literal meaning: "One worthy of worship," it is a technical term designating abstract principles and a variety of old Indo-European gods and goddesses who were incorporated into the pantheon of the Good Religion under Ahura Mazda. They are widely referred to as "angels" as they are transmitters of the will of the divine godhead. It is from this tradition that the doctrine of angels was developed in the Judaic, Christian and Muslim religions.

CPSIA information can be obtained
at www.ICGtesting.com
Printed in the USA
BVHW032344080720
583189BV00002B/327